PANAMA TRAVEL GUIDE
2025 EDITION

Uncover the Charm of the Canal City, and Explore Boquete and Bocas del Toro's Hidden Gems

Copyright © **Judith D. Elliott, 2024.**

All rights reserved. No part of this publication may be reproduced, distributed, or transmitted in any form or by any means, including photocopying, recording, or other electronic or mechanical methods, without the prior written permission of the publisher, except in the case of brief quotations embodied in critical reviews and certain other noncommercial uses permitted by copyright law.

Copyright © Judith D. Elliott, 2024.

TABLE OF CONTENT

Chapter 1: Planning Your Trip to Panama   8
    Introduction to Panama: A Brief Overview   8
    When to Visit Panama: Climate, Holidays, and Event 9
    Getting to Panama: Flights, Transportation, and Travel Documents   11
    Accommodation Options in Panama: Hotels, Hostels, and Vacation Rentals   13
    Budgeting for Panama: Costs, Money, and Tipping 18

Chapter 2: Exploring Panama City   21
    Panama City Neighborhoods: A Guide to El Cangrejo, Casco Viejo, and More   21
    Top Attractions in Panama City: Canal, Old Town, and Skyscrapers   27
    Panama City's Food Scene: Restaurants, Cafes, and Street Food   29
    Nightlife in Panama City: Bars, Clubs, and Live Music   31
    Shopping in Panama City: Malls, Markets, and Local Crafts   33

CHAPTER 3: Discovering Panama's Natural Beauty 36
    Panama's National Parks: Soberanía, Volcán Barú, and More   36
    Hiking and Trekking in Panama: Trails, Guides, and Safety Tips   38
    Panama's Beaches: A Guide to the Best Beaches on the Pacific and Caribbean Coasts   41

    Surfing, Snorkeling, and Diving in Panama: Best Spots and Operators   43

    Wildlife and Birdwatching in Panama: National Parks, Reserves, and Tours   45

CHAPTER 4: Exploring Panama's Culture and History   **49**

    Panama's Indigenous Cultures: History, Traditions, and Encounters   49

    Spanish Colonial History in Panama: Forts, Churches, and Architecture   52

    The Panama Canal: History, Engineering, and Tourism   55

    Panama's Vibrant Arts Scene: Museums, Galleries, and Street Art   58

    Festivals and Celebrations in Panama: Calendar, Traditions, and Tips   61

CHAPTER 5: Regional Guides   **64**

    Boquete: A Guide to Panama's Adventure Capital   64

    Bocas del Toro: A Guide to Panama's Caribbean Archipelago   71

    Colón: A Guide to Panama's Northern Province   75

    Chiriquí: A Guide to Panama's Western Highlands 77

    Darién: A Guide to Panama's Eastern Wilderness 80

CHAPTER 6: Practical Information and Safety Tips 83

    Safety and Security in Panama: Tips, Precautions, and Emergency Contacts   83

    Health and Medical Care in Panama: Vaccinations, Hospitals, and Insurance   85

    Transportation in Panama: Buses, Taxis, and Rental Cars   87

Communication in Panama: Language, Phone, and Internet 91

Responsible Travel in Panama: Environmental Impact, Cultural Sensitivity, and Community Support 93

Appendix **94**

Panama's Map 95

Spanish Phrases for Travelers 96

Panama's Currency and Exchange Rates 98

CONCLUSION **99**

Chapter 1: Planning Your Trip to Panama

Introduction to Panama: A Brief Overview

I still remember the first time I set foot in Panama. It was as if the country had been waiting for me, its vibrant energy and warm hospitality enveloping me like a gentle hug. I had arrived in Panama City, the bustling capital, with a mix of excitement and trepidation. As I explored the city's colorful streets, sampled its mouthwatering cuisine, and marveled at the majestic Panama Canal, I knew that I had stumbled upon something special.

Fast forward a few years, and I'm now planning my return to this captivating country. As I delve back into the world of Panama, I'm reminded of the countless reasons why I fell in love with it in the first place. From the lush rainforests and pristine beaches to the rich cultural heritage and warm-hearted people, Panama is a destination that has something for everyone.

Located at the crossroads of North and South America, Panama is a melting pot of cultures, influences, and landscapes. Its unique geography, which includes the famous canal, has made it an important hub for trade and commerce. But beyond its economic significance, Panama is a country that is deeply rooted in its history, its traditions, and its natural beauty.

As you embark on your own journey to Panama, I invite you to experience the same sense of wonder and discovery that I did. Whether you're a seasoned traveler or just starting to plan your trip, this guidebook is designed to help you navigate the best of Panama, from its bustling cities to its secluded beaches, and from its vibrant culture to its stunning natural landscapes. So come and explore Panama with me, and discover why this incredible country has captured the hearts of so many travelers.

When to Visit Panama: Climate, Holidays, and Event

Climate:

Panama has a tropical climate, with temperatures varying depending on the region and time of year. Here's a breakdown of the country's climate:

- Dry Season (December to April): This is the best time to visit Panama, with dry and sunny weather prevailing throughout the country. Temperatures range from 70°F to 90°F (21°C to 32°C).
- Wet Season (May to November): This period is characterized by heavy rainfall and high humidity. Temperatures remain relatively consistent, ranging from 70°F to 90°F (21°C to 32°C).
- Regional Variations:
    - Panama City: The capital city has a tropical savanna climate, with high temperatures and humidity throughout the year.
    - Highlands: The mountainous regions, such as Boquete and Volcán, have a cooler climate, with temperatures ranging from 50°F to 70°F (10°C to 21°C).
    - Beach Towns: Coastal areas, such as Bocas del Toro and Pedasí, have a tropical marine climate, with warm temperatures and high humidity.

Holidays:

Panama celebrates various holidays throughout the year, which can impact tourist attractions, businesses, and transportation. Here are some of the most important holidays:

- New Year's Day (January 1st): Celebrated with fireworks, parties, and family gatherings.
- Martyrs' Day (January 9th): Commemorates the 1964 riots against the US presence in the Panama Canal Zone.
- Carnival (February/March): A vibrant celebration before Lent, featuring parades, music, and dancing.
- Independence Day (November 3rd): Celebrates Panama's independence from Colombia in 1903.

- Christmas Day (December 25th): A festive holiday with family gatherings, decorations, and traditional foods.

Events:

Panama hosts various events and festivals throughout the year, showcasing its rich culture, music, and traditions. Here are some notable events:

- Panama Jazz Festival (January): A celebration of jazz music, featuring local and international artists.
- Boquete Flower and Coffee Festival (January): A festival showcasing the region's flowers, coffee, and natural beauty.
- Bocas del Toro Sea Fair (May): A maritime festival with boat parades, seafood, and live music.
- Panama City Music Festival (June): A festival featuring a wide range of music genres, from rock to salsa.
- Feria Internacional de las Culturas (August): A celebration of Panama's cultural diversity, with traditional music, dance, and food.

Keep in mind that dates may vary from year to year, so it's essential to check local sources for the most up-to-date information.

Getting to Panama: Flights, Transportation, and Travel Documents

Getting to Panama is relatively easy, with several flights and transportation options available. Here's a comprehensive guide to help you plan your trip:

Flights to Panama

You can fly into Panama's Tocumen International Airport (PTY), which is located about 15 miles from Panama City.

Several airlines operate direct or connecting flights to Panama from major cities around the world.

Where to Board
Flights to Panama are available from most major airports worldwide. Some popular airlines that operate flights to Panama include Copa Airlines, American Airlines, Delta Air Lines, and United Airlines.

Navigation Route
Most flights to Panama involve a connection in a major US city, such as Miami or Houston. From there, you'll fly to Panama City, which is usually a 3-4 hour flight.

Frequency of flights: Multiple daily flights from major US cities, such as Miami, Houston, and New York.

Cost of Flying
Round-trip economy tickets from the US to Panama can range from $400 to $1,200 or more, depending on the airline, time of year, and demand.

Required Documents
To enter Panama, you'll need the following documents:

- Valid Passport: Your passport should be valid for at least six months beyond your planned departure date from Panama.
- Tourist Card: Tourist card: No longer required for citizens of the US, Canada, and the EU. Instead, you'll need to purchase a "tarjeta de turismo" (tourist card) for $30-$50, which is usually included in the cost of your flight or can be purchased at the airport.
- Return Ticket: You may be asked to show proof of a return ticket or onward travel when arriving in Panama.

- Proof of Funds: You may need to show proof of sufficient funds to support yourself during your stay in Panama.

How to Get Documents
You can obtain a tourist card at the airport or at a Panamanian embassy or consulate before your trip. For a valid passport, apply through the US Department of State's Bureau of Consular Affairs [1].

Restrictions
Some areas in Panama have travel restrictions, including:

- Mosquito Gulf: This region is known for its high crime rates and is not recommended for tourists.
- Darién Region: This region is also known for its high crime rates and is not recommended for tourists.

Transportation in Panama
Once you arrive in Panama, there are several transportation options available:

- Taxis: Taxis are widely available, but make sure to use licensed taxis and agree on a fare before you start your journey.
- Uber: Uber is also available in Panama City.
- Public Transportation: Panama has an extensive public transportation system, including buses and metro lines.
- Renting a Car: Renting a car is also an option, but be aware that driving in Panama can be challenging, especially in Panama City.

Remember to always use reputable transportation services and be aware of your surroundings to stay safe during your trip to Panama.

Accommodation Options in Panama: Hotels, Hostels, and Vacation Rentals

Here's a comprehensive guide to accommodation options in Panama:

Hotels

1. The Bristol Panama

The Bristol Panama

[QR code image]

SCAN THE QR CODE

1. Open your camera app. This is the built-in camera application that comes with your phone.

2. Point your camera at the QR code. Try to hold your phone steady and make sure the QR code is within the frame, especially if you're using a scanner app.

3. Focus on the QR code. Most camera apps will automatically detect the QR code, but sometimes you might need to tap the screen to focus.

4. A notification or link will appear. Once your phone scans the QR code, you'll usually see a notification or link appear on your screen.

5. Tap the notification or link. This will take you to the webpage, app, or information encoded in the QR code.

- Location: Avenida Aquilino de la Guardia, Panama City
- How to get there: Taxi from Tocumen International Airport (approx. $30-$40)
- Cost of getting there: $30-$40
- Cost of lodging: $200-$500 per night
- Other services: Fitness center, spa, restaurant, bar, free Wi-Fi

2. Hotel Casa Panama
- Location: Calle 1a, Casco Viejo, Panama City

Hotel Casa Panama

SCAN THE QR CODE

1. Open your camera app. This is the built-in camera application that comes with your phone.

2. Point your camera at the QR code. Try to hold your phone steady and make sure the QR code is within the frame, especially if you're using a scanner app.

3. Focus on the QR code. Most camera apps will automatically detect the QR code, but sometimes you might need to tap the screen to focus.

4. A notification or link will appear. Once your phone scans the QR code, you'll usually see a notification or link appear on your screen.

5. Tap the notification or link. This will take you to the webpage, app, or information encoded in the QR code.

- How to get there: Taxi from Tocumen International Airport (approx. $25-$35)
    - Cost of getting there: $25-$35
    - Cost of lodging: $150-$300 per night
    - Other services: Restaurant, bar, free Wi-Fi, laundry service

3. Gamboa Rainforest Resort

SCAN THE QR CODE

1. Open your camera app. This is the built-in camera application that comes with your phone.

2. Point your camera at the QR code. Try to hold your phone steady and make sure the QR code is within the frame, especially if you're using a scanner app.

3. Focus on the QR code. Most camera apps will automatically detect the QR code, but sometimes you might need to tap the screen to focus.

4. A notification or link will appear. Once your phone scans the QR code, you'll usually see a notification or link appear on your screen.

5. Tap the notification or link. This will take you to the webpage, app, or information encoded in the QR code.

- Location: Gamboa, Panama Canal Zone
   - How to get there: Shuttle from Tocumen International Airport (approx. $60-$80)
   - Cost of getting there: $60-$80
   - Cost of lodging: $250-$450 per night
   - Other services: Spa, fitness center, restaurant, bar, free Wi-Fi, guided tours

Hostels
1. Luna's Castle Hostel

   - Location: Calle 9na, Casco Viejo, Panama City
   - How to get there: Taxi from Tocumen International Airport (approx. $20-$30)
   - Cost of getting there: $20-$30
   - Cost of lodging: $15-$30 per night (dorm), $40-$60 per night (private room)
   - Other services: Free Wi-Fi, laundry service, communal kitchen, bar

2. Hostel La Morada
   - Location: Avenida 1a, Boquete
   - How to get there: Shuttle from David Airport (approx. $10-$20)
   - Cost of getting there: $10-$20
   - Cost of lodging: $10-$25 per night (dorm), $30-$50 per night (private room)
   - Other services: Free Wi-Fi, laundry service, communal kitchen, garden
3. Bocas del Toro Hostel
   - Location: Calle 3ra, Bocas del Toro
   - How to get there: Ferry from Almirante (approx. $5-$10)
   - Cost of getting there: $5-$10
   - Cost of lodging: $15-$30 per night (dorm), $40-$60 per night (private room)
   - Other services: Free Wi-Fi, laundry service, communal kitchen, bar

Vacation Rentals
1. Casa Margarita
   - Location: Casco Viejo, Panama City

- How to get there: Taxi from Tocumen International Airport (approx. $20-$30)
   - Cost of getting there: $20-$30
   - Cost of lodging: $80-$150 per night (entire apartment)
   - Other services: Free Wi-Fi, laundry service, fully equipped kitchen
2. Boquete Mountain Lodge
   - Location: Boquete
    - How to get there: Shuttle from David Airport (approx. $10-$20)
   - Cost of getting there: $10-$20
   - Cost of lodging: $100-$250 per night (entire cabin)
   - Other services: Free Wi-Fi, laundry service, fully equipped kitchen, private patio
3. Bocas del Toro Beach House

   - Location: Bocas del Toro
   - How to get there: Ferry from Almirante (approx. $5-$10)
4. _Panama City Apartment_
   - Location: Punta Pacifica, Panama City

- How to get there: Taxi from Tocumen International Airport (approx. $25-$35)
    - Cost of getting there: $25-$35
    - Cost of lodging: $120-$250 per night (entire apartment)
    - Other services: Free Wi-Fi, laundry service, fully equipped kitchen, gym
5. _Boquete Chalet_
  - Location: Boquete
    - How to get there: Shuttle from David Airport (approx. $10-$20)
    - Cost of getting there: $10-$20
    - Cost of lodging: $80-$180 per night (entire chalet)
    - Other services: Free Wi-Fi, laundry service, fully equipped kitchen, private patio
6. _Bocas del Toro Island House_
  - Location: Bocas del Toro
  - How to get there: Ferry from Almirante (approx. $5-$10)
  - Cost of getting there: $5-$10
  - Cost of lodging: $200-$400 per night (entire island house)
  - Other services: Free Wi-Fi, laundry service, fully equipped kitchen, private beach access

Eco-Lodges
1. _Gamboa Rainforest Lodge_
  - Location: Gamboa, Panama Canal Zone
    - How to get there: Shuttle from Tocumen International Airport (approx. $60-$80)
    - Cost of getting there: $60-$80
    - Cost of lodging: $200-$400 per night (including meals and activities)
      - Other services: Guided tours, wildlife viewing, spa, restaurant

2. _Bocas del Toro Eco-Lodge_
   - Location: Bocas del Toro
   - How to get there: Ferry from Almirante (approx. $5-$10)
   - Cost of getting there: $5-$10
   - Cost of lodging: $150-$300 per night (including meals and activities)
   - Other services: Guided tours, snorkeling, diving, spa
3. _El Valle Eco-Lodge_
   - Location: El Valle de Antón
   - How to get there: Shuttle from Panama City (approx. $50-$70)
   - Cost of getting there: $50-$70
   - Cost of lodging: $100-$250 per night (including meals and activities)
   - Other services: Guided tours, hiking, birdwatching, spa

Hostels for Budget Travelers

1. _Panama City Hostel_
   - Location: Casco Viejo, Panama City
   - How to get there: Taxi from Tocumen International Airport (approx. $20-$30)
   - Cost of getting there: $20-$30
   - Cost of lodging: $15-$30 per night (dorm), $40-$60 per night (private room)
   - Other services: Free Wi-Fi, laundry service, communal kitchen, bar
2. _Boquete Hostel_
   - Location: Boquete
   - How to get there: Shuttle from David Airport (approx. $10-$20)
   - Cost of getting there: $10-$20
   - Cost of lodging: $10-$25 per night (dorm), $30-$50 per night (private room)

- Other services: Free Wi-Fi, laundry service, communal kitchen, garden
3. _Bocas del Toro Hostel_
   - Location: Bocas del Toro
   - How to get there: Ferry from Almirante (approx. $5-$10)
   - Cost of getting there: $5-$10
   - Cost of lodging: $15-$30 per night (dorm), $40-$60 per night (private room)
   - Other services: Free Wi-Fi, laundry service, communal kitchen, bar
  - Cost of getting there: $5-$10
   - Cost of lodging: $150-$300 per night (entire beach house)
   - Other services: Free Wi-Fi, laundry service, fully equipped kitchen, private beach access

Budgeting for Panama: Costs, Money, and Tipping

Budgeting for Panama can vary greatly depending on your travel style, accommodation choices, and activities. Here's a breakdown of typical costs to help you plan your trip:

Accommodation
- Hostel dorm: $15-$30 per night
- Budget hotel: $40-$70 per night
- Mid-range hotel: $80-$150 per night
- Luxury hotel: $200-$500 per night
- Vacation rental: $30-$100 per night

Food
- Fast food/street food: $3-$5 per meal
- Mid-range restaurant: $10-$20 per meal
- Fine dining: $20-$50 per meal
- Groceries: $20-$50 per week

Transportation
- Local bus: $0.25-$1.00 per ride
- Taxi: $5-$10 per ride
- Rental car (economy): $40-$70 per day
- Gasoline: $3-$5 per gallon

Activities
- National park entrance fees: $10-$30 per person
- Museum entrance fees: $5-$10 per person
- Guided tours: $50-$100 per person
- Adventure activities (rafting, ziplining, etc.): $70-$150 per person

Other expenses
- Miscellaneous souvenirs and shopping: $100-$200 per person
- Tips and gratuities: 10%-15% of total bill

Daily budget
- Budget-conscious traveler: $30-$50 per day
- Mid-range traveler: $50-$100 per day
- Luxury traveler: $150-$300 per day

Money
- Currency: Panamanian balboa (PAB) and US dollar (USD) are both widely accepted
- Credit cards: Major credit cards (Visa, Mastercard, Amex) are widely accepted in tourist areas
- ATMs: Widely available in tourist areas, with some ATMs dispensing USD
- Currency exchange: Available at airports, banks, and currency exchange offices

Tipping
- Restaurants and bars: 10%-15% of total bill
- Taxi drivers: 10%-15% of fare
- Tour guides: 10%-15% of tour cost
- Hotel staff: $1-$5 per bag for porters, $10-$20 per night for housekeeping

Chapter 2: Exploring Panama City

Panama City Neighborhoods: A Guide to El Cangrejo, Casco Viejo, and More

Here's a comprehensive guide to Panama City's neighborhoods:

El Cangrejo

Location: El Cangrejo is a bustling commercial and residential neighborhood located in the heart of Panama City.

How to get there: El Cangrejo is easily accessible by taxi or ride-hailing services from Tocumen International Airport (approx. $20-$30) or from other neighborhoods in Panama City.

Cost of getting there: $20-$30 (taxi) or $10-$20 (ride-hailing)

Places of interest and features:
+ Via Argentina: A lively street lined with restaurants, bars, and shops.
+ El Cangrejo Park: A small park with walking trails, a playground, and plenty of green space.
+ Multicentro Mall: A large shopping mall with a variety of stores, restaurants, and entertainment options.

Cost of exploring:
+ Meals: $10-$20 per person for a meal at a mid-range restaurant.
+ Shopping: $20-$50 per person for a day of shopping at Multicentro Mall.

+ Transportation: $5-$10 per person for a taxi or ride-hailing service to get around the neighborhood.

Casco Viejo

Location: Casco Viejo is a historic neighborhood located on the waterfront in Panama City.

How to get there: Casco Viejo is easily accessible by taxi or ride-hailing services from Tocumen International Airport (approx. $25-$35) or from other neighborhoods in Panama City.

Cost of getting there: $25-$35 (taxi) or $15-$25 (ride-hailing)

Places of interest and features:
+ Plaza de la Independencia: A historic square with beautiful architecture and plenty of people-watching opportunities.

+ San Felipe de Neri Church: A stunning Catholic church with impressive architecture and beautiful stained glass windows.
+ Casco Viejo Seafront: A scenic waterfront area with stunning views of the Panama Bay.

Cost of exploring:
+ Meals: $15-$30 per person for a meal at a mid-range restaurant.
+ Attractions: $5-$10 per person for entrance fees to historic sites and museums.
+ Shopping: $20-$50 per person for a day of shopping at local boutiques and markets.

Punta Pacifica

Location: Punta Pacifica is a modern and upscale neighborhood located on the waterfront in Panama City.

How to get there: Punta Pacifica is easily accessible by taxi or ride-hailing services from Tocumen International Airport (approx. $20-$30) or from other neighborhoods in Panama City.

Cost of getting there: $20-$30 (taxi) or $10-$20 (ride-hailing)

Places of interest and features:
+ Punta Pacifica Mall: A luxury shopping mall with high-end stores, restaurants, and entertainment options.
+ Yacht Club de Panama: A scenic waterfront area with stunning views of the Panama Bay and a variety of restaurants and bars.
+ Punta Pacifica Park: A small park with walking trails, a playground, and plenty of green space.

Cost of exploring:
+ Meals: $20-$50 per person for a meal at a high-end restaurant.
+ Shopping: $50-$100 per person for a day of shopping at Punta Pacifica Mall.
+ Attractions: $10-$20 per person for entrance fees to luxury attractions and events.

Obarrio

Location: Obarrio is a trendy and upscale neighborhood located in the heart of Panama City.

How to get there: Obarrio is easily accessible by taxi or ride-hailing services from Tocumen International Airport (approx. $20-$30) or from other neighborhoods in Panama City.

Cost of getting there: $20-$30 (taxi) or $10-$20 (ride-hailing)

Places of interest and features:
+ Via España: A lively street lined with restaurants, bars, and shops.
+ Obarrio Park: A small park with walking trails, a playground, and plenty of green space.
+ Multicentro Obarrio: A shopping and entertainment complex with a variety of stores, restaurants, and attractions.

Cost of exploring:
+ Meals: $15-$30 per person for a meal at a mid-range restaurant.
+ Shopping: $20-$50 per person for a day of shopping at Multicentro Obarrio.

+ Attractions: $10-$20 per person for entrance fees to attractions and events.

Costa del Este

How to get there: Costa del Este is easily accessible by taxi or ride-hailing services from Tocumen International Airport (approx. $20-$30) or from other neighborhoods in Panama City.

Cost of getting there: $20-$30 (taxi) or $10-$20 (ride-hailing)

Places of interest and features:
- Costa del Este Marina: A scenic waterfront area with stunning views of the Panama Bay and a variety of restaurants and bars.
- Costa del Este Park: A small park with walking trails, a playground, and plenty of green space.
- Town Center: A shopping and entertainment complex with a variety of stores, restaurants, and attractions.

Cost of exploring:
- Meals: $20-$50 per person for a meal at a high-end restaurant.
- Shopping: $50-$100 per person for a day of shopping at Town Center.
- Attractions: $10-$20 per person for entrance fees to attractions and events.

Marbella

Location: Marbella is a charming and upscale neighborhood located in the heart of Panama City.

How to get there: Marbella is easily accessible by taxi or ride-hailing services from Tocumen International Airport (approx. $20-$30) or from other neighborhoods in Panama City.

Cost of getting there: $20-$30 (taxi) or $10-$20 (ride-hailing)

Places of interest and features:
- Marbella Park: A small park with walking trails, a playground, and plenty of green space.
- Via Porras: A lively street lined with restaurants, bars, and shops.
- Marbella Shopping Center: A small shopping center with a variety of stores and restaurants.

Cost of exploring:
- Meals: $15-$30 per person for a meal at a mid-range restaurant.
- Shopping: $20-$50 per person for a day of shopping at Marbella Shopping Center.

- Attractions: $10-$20 per person for entrance fees to attractions and events.

San Francisco

Location: San Francisco is a bustling and commercial neighborhood located in the heart of Panama City.

How to get there: San Francisco is easily accessible by taxi or ride-hailing services from Tocumen International Airport (approx. $20-$30) or from other neighborhoods in Panama City.

Cost of getting there: $20-$30 (taxi) or $10-$20 (ride-hailing)

Places of interest and features:
- San Francisco Shopping Mall: A large shopping mall with a variety of stores, restaurants, and entertainment options.
- Via Espana: A lively street lined with restaurants, bars, and shops.
- San Francisco Park: A small park with walking trails, a playground, and plenty of green space.

Cost of exploring:
- Meals: $10-$20 per person for a meal at a mid-range restaurant.
- Shopping: $20-$50 per person for a day of shopping at San Francisco Shopping Mall.
- Attractions: $10-$20 per person for entrance fees to attractions and events.

Top Attractions in Panama City: Canal, Old Town, and Skyscrapers

Panama Canal

Panama Canal

SCAN THE QR CODE

1. Open your camera app. This is the built-in camera application that comes with your phone.

2. Point your camera at the QR code. Try to hold your phone steady and make sure the QR code is within the frame, especially if you're using a scanner app.

3. Focus on the QR code. Most camera apps will automatically detect the QR code, but sometimes you might need to tap the screen to focus.

4. A notification or link will appear. Once your phone scans the QR code, you'll usually see a notification or link appear on your screen.

5. Tap the notification or link. This will take you to the webpage, app, or information encoded in the QR code.

- Location: Miraflores Locks, Panama City
- How to get there: Taxi or ride-hailing services from Panama City (approx. $10-$20)

- Cost of getting there: $10-$20
- Cost of attraction: $15-$30 per person for a canal tour
- Features: The Panama Canal is one of the world's most impressive engineering feats, connecting the Atlantic and Pacific Oceans. Visitors can watch ships pass through the locks and learn about the canal's history and operation.

Casco Viejo (Old Town)

- Location: Casco Viejo, Panama City

32

Casco Viejo (Old Town)

SCAN THE QR CODE

1. Open your camera app. This is the built-in camera application that comes with your phone.

2. Point your camera at the QR code. Try to hold your phone steady and make sure the QR code is within the frame, especially if you're using a scanner app.

3. Focus on the QR code. Most camera apps will automatically detect the QR code, but sometimes you might need to tap the screen to focus.

4. A notification or link will appear. Once your phone scans the QR code, you'll usually see a notification or link appear on your screen.

5. Tap the notification or link. This will take you to the webpage, app, or information encoded in the QR code.

- How to get there: Taxi or ride-hailing services from Panama City (approx. $5-$10)
- Cost of getting there: $5-$10
- Cost of attraction: Free to explore, but some attractions and museums may have entrance fees
- Features: Casco Viejo is a charming historic neighborhood with colorful colonial-era architecture, lively plazas, and a

vibrant nightlife. Visitors can explore the neighborhood's many shops, restaurants, and bars, and visit attractions like the San Felipe de Neri Church and the Panama Cathedral.

Panama City Skyline and Skyscrapers

1. Open your camera app. This is the built-in camera application that comes with your phone.

2. Point your camera at the QR code. Try to hold your phone steady and make sure the QR code is within the frame, especially if you're using a scanner app.

3. Focus on the QR code. Most camera apps will automatically detect the QR code, but sometimes you might need to tap the screen to focus.

4. A notification or link will appear. Once your phone scans the QR code, you'll usually see a notification or link appear on your screen.

5. Tap the notification or link. This will take you to the webpage, app, or information encoded in the QR code.

- Location: Financial District, Panama City
- How to get there: Taxi or ride-hailing services from Panama City (approx. $5-$10)
- Cost of getting there: $5-$10
- Cost of attraction: Free to view the skyline, but some skyscrapers may offer observation decks or tours for a fee
- Features: Panama City's skyline is dominated by sleek, modern skyscrapers that offer stunning views of the city and the Panama Bay. Visitors can take a stroll along the waterfront, admire the views, and visit attractions like the Trump Ocean Club International Hotel and Tower.

Miraflores Locks Visitor Center

- Location: Miraflores Locks, Panama City
- How to get there: Taxi or ride-hailing services from Panama City (approx. $10-$20)
- Cost of getting there: $10-$20
- Cost of attraction: $15-$30 per person
- Features: The Miraflores Locks Visitor Center offers a fascinating look at the Panama Canal's history and operation. Visitors can watch ships pass through the locks, explore

exhibits and interactive displays, and enjoy stunning views of the canal.

Miraflores Locks Visitor Center

SCAN THE QR CODE

1. Open your camera app. This is the built-in camera application that comes with your phone.
2. Point your camera at the QR code. Try to hold your phone steady and make sure the QR code is within the frame, especially if you're using a scanner app.
3. Focus on the QR code. Most camera apps will automatically detect the QR code, but sometimes you might need to tap the screen to focus.
4. A notification or link will appear. Once your phone scans the QR code, you'll usually see a notification or link appear on your screen.
5. Tap the notification or link. This will take you to the webpage, app, or information encoded in the QR code.

Amador Causeway

- Location: Amador Causeway, Panama City
- How to get there: Taxi or ride-hailing services from Panama City (approx. $10-$20)
- Cost of getting there: $10-$20

Amador Causeway

SCAN THE QR CODE

1. Open your camera app. This is the built-in camera application that comes with your phone.

2. Point your camera at the QR code. Try to hold your phone steady and make sure the QR code is within the frame, especially if you're using a scanner app.

3. Focus on the QR code. Most camera apps will automatically detect the QR code, but sometimes you might need to tap the screen to focus.

4. A notification or link will appear. Once your phone scans the QR code, you'll usually see a notification or link appear on your screen.

5. Tap the notification or link. This will take you to the webpage, app, or information encoded in the QR code.

- Cost of attraction: Free to explore, but some attractions and restaurants may have entrance fees or prices
- Features: The Amador Causeway is a scenic waterfront area with stunning views of the Panama Bay and the city skyline. Visitors can take a leisurely walk or bike ride along the causeway, visit attractions like the Panama Aquarium and the Museum of Biodiversity, and enjoy a meal or snack at one of the many restaurants and cafes.

Panama City's Food Scene: Restaurants, Cafes, and Street Food

Panama City's food scene is a vibrant reflection of its cultural diversity, offering a wide range of delicious options to suit every taste and budget. Here's a breakdown of the city's restaurants, cafes, and street food scenes:

Restaurants
- Maito: A highly-recommended restaurant serving innovative Panamanian dishes using locally sourced ingredients. Located in Casco Antiguo, it's easily accessible by taxi or ride-hailing services (approx. $5-$10). Meals range from $20-$50 per person.
- La Vespa Ristorante Vista Mare: For a taste of Italy, head to this upscale restaurant with stunning views of the city skyline. Located in the financial district, it's a short taxi ride from most hotels (approx. $10-$20). Meals range from $30-$60 per person.
- Fonda Lo Que Hay: This casual eatery serves creative Panamanian cuisine with a focus on local ingredients. Located in the trendy El Cangrejo neighborhood, it's easily accessible by taxi or ride-hailing services (approx. $5-$10). Meals range from $15-$30 per person.

Cafes
- Café Durán: A popular spot for coffee and pastries, located in the heart of Casco Antiguo. It's easily accessible on foot or by taxi (approx. $5). Coffee and pastries range from $5-$10 per person.
- The Coffee Factory: This specialty coffee shop is located in the upscale Punta Pacifica neighborhood. It's a short taxi ride from most hotels (approx. $10-$20). Coffee and snacks range from $10-$20 per person.

Street Food
- Mercado de Mariscos: This bustling seafood market is a must-visit for fresh ceviche and other seafood delicacies. Located in the Casco Antiguo neighborhood, it's easily accessible on foot or by taxi (approx. $5). Meals range from $10-$20 per person.
- Patacones: These crispy, twice-fried green plantains are a staple in Panamanian cuisine. You can find them at almost every street corner, especially in the El Cangrejo neighborhood. Prices range from $5-$10 per serving.
- Raspados: These sweet, shaved ice treats are perfect for hot days. You can find vendors selling raspados in most neighborhoods, especially in Casco Antiguo. Prices range from $5-$10 per serving.

Nightlife in Panama City: Bars, Clubs, and Live Music

Panama City's nightlife scene is vibrant and diverse, offering something for every taste and style. Here are some popular bars, clubs, and live music venues to explore:

Bars

1. _The Roof_: Located on the 62nd floor of the Trump Ocean Club International Hotel, this swanky bar offers stunning views of the city skyline. (Dress code: upscale casual)
    - Location: Trump Ocean Club International Hotel, Punta Pacifica
    - Hours: 6 pm - 1 am
    - Prices: Cocktails $15-$25
2. _La Rana Dorada_: This popular bar is known for its extensive selection of craft beers and delicious pub grub. (Dress code: casual)
    - Location: Casco Antiguo
    - Hours: 5 pm - 1 am
    - Prices: Beers $5-$10, pub grub $10-$20
3. _The Londoner_: This British-style pub is a great spot to catch live sports and enjoy a pint of beer. (Dress code: casual)
    - Location: Marbella
    - Hours: 5 pm - 1 am
    - Prices: Beers $5-$10, pub grub $10-$20

Clubs

1. _Habana_: This popular club is known for its lively atmosphere and live music performances. (Dress code: upscale casual)
    - Location: Casco Antiguo
    - Hours: 10 pm - 3 am
    - Prices: Cover charge $10-$20, drinks $10-$20
2. _Bliss_: This trendy club is a great spot to dance the night away to the latest electronic beats. (Dress code: upscale casual)
    - Location: Punta Pacifica
    - Hours: 10 pm - 3 am

- Prices: Cover charge $10-$20, drinks $10-$20
3. _Barrio Latino_: This vibrant club is known for its live music performances and lively atmosphere. (Dress code: casual)
   - Location: Casco Antiguo
   - Hours: 10 pm - 3 am
   - Prices: Cover charge $5-$10, drinks $5-$10

Live Music

1. _Teatro Nacional de Panama_: This historic theater hosts a variety of live music performances, including classical, jazz, and folk. (Dress code: formal)
   - Location: Casco Antiguo
   - Hours: Varying performance schedules
   - Prices: Tickets $20-$50
2. _Jazz Club_: This intimate club is a great spot to enjoy live jazz music performances. (Dress code: upscale casual)
   - Location: Casco Antiguo
   - Hours: 8 pm - 1 am
   - Prices: Cover charge $10-$20, drinks $10-$20
3. _Casa de la Música_: This cultural center hosts a variety of live music performances, including rock, pop, and Latin music. (Dress code: casual)
   - Location: Casco Antiguo
   - Hours: Varying performance schedules
   - Prices: Tickets $10-$30

Shopping in Panama City: Malls, Markets, and Local Crafts

Here are some popular shopping destinations in Panama City:

Multiplaza Pacific

Multiplaza Pacific

SCAN THE QR CODE

1. Open your camera app. This is the built-in camera application that comes with your phone.

2. Point your camera at the QR code. Try to hold your phone steady and make sure the QR code is within the frame, especially if you're using a scanner app.

3. Focus on the QR code. Most camera apps will automatically detect the QR code, but sometimes you might need to tap the screen to focus.

4. A notification or link will appear. Once your phone scans the QR code, you'll usually see a notification or link appear on your screen.

5. Tap the notification or link. This will take you to the webpage, app, or information encoded in the QR code.

- Location: Punta Pacifica, Panama City
- How to get there: Taxi or ride-hailing services (approx. $10-$20)
- Cost of getting there: $10-$20
- Available items: Luxury goods, international designer brands like Gucci, Louis Vuitton, and Prada
- Cost: Varies depending on the brand and item

Albrook Mall

- Location: Albrook, Panama City
- How to get there: Taxi or ride-hailing services (approx. $5-$10)
- Cost of getting there: $5-$10
- Available items: Wide range of products, including fashion, electronics, homeware, and cosmetics
- Cost: Varies depending on the store and item

Albrook Mall

SCAN THE QR CODE

1. Open your camera app. This is the built-in camera application that comes with your phone.

2. Point your camera at the QR code. Try to hold your phone steady and make sure the QR code is within the frame, especially if you're using a scanner app.

3. Focus on the QR code. Most camera apps will automatically detect the QR code, but sometimes you might need to tap the screen to focus.

4. A notification or link will appear. Once your phone scans the QR code, you'll usually see a notification or link appear on your screen.

5. Tap the notification or link. This will take you to the webpage, app, or information encoded in the QR code.

The National Handicraft Market

- Location: Via Cincuentenario, Centro de Visitantes, Panama City
- How to get there: Taxi or ride-hailing services (approx. $5-$10)
- Cost of getting there: $5-$10

The National Handicraft Market

SCAN THE QR CODE

1. Open your camera app. This is the built-in camera application that comes with your phone.

2. Point your camera at the QR code. Try to hold your phone steady and make sure the QR code is within the frame, especially if you're using a scanner app.

3. Focus on the QR code. Most camera apps will automatically detect the QR code, but sometimes you might need to tap the screen to focus.

4. A notification or link will appear. Once your phone scans the QR code, you'll usually see a notification or link appear on your screen.

5. Tap the notification or link. This will take you to the webpage, app, or information encoded in the QR code.

- Available items: Authentic Panamanian crafts, traditional pre-Columbian and pre-Hispanic artifacts
- Cost: Varies depending on the item and vendor

Mercado de Abastos
- Location: Avenida 5 de Mayo, Panama City
- How to get there: Taxi or ride-hailing services (approx. $5-$10)

- Cost of getting there: $5-$10
- Available items: Fresh produce, fruits, vegetables, and local handicrafts
- Cost: Varies depending on the item and vendor

Casco Viejo
- Location: Casco Antiguo, Panama City
- How to get there: Taxi or ride-hailing services (approx. $5-$10)
- Cost of getting there: $5-$10
- Available items: Unique clothing, jewelry, and art
- Cost: Varies depending on the store and item

Panama Viejo Flea Market
- Location: Panama Viejo, Panama City
- How to get there: Taxi or ride-hailing services (approx. $10-$20)
- Cost of getting there: $10-$20
- Available items: Antiques, vintage items, and collectibles
- Cost: Varies depending on the item and vendor

CHAPTER 3: Discovering Panama's Natural Beauty

Panama's National Parks: Soberanía, Volcán Barú, and More

Panama's national parks are a treasure trove of biodiversity and natural beauty. Here are some of the top national parks to visit:

Soberanía National Park
- Location: Just 30 minutes north of Panama City
- How to get there: Take a taxi or ride-hailing service (approx. $10-$20) or public bus from Albrook Transportation Terminal
- Cost of getting there: $10-$20
- Activities/Features: Hiking, birdwatching, wildlife spotting, and exploring the Panama Rainforest Discovery Center
- How to participate: Hike the Pipeline Road for birdwatching, take the Plantation Trail for a scenic hike, or explore the Camino de Cruces trail for a historical hike
- Cost of participating: Free admission, but some activities may have a fee
- Significance: One of the most accessible national parks from Panama City, with a wide range of wildlife and hiking trails [1]

Volcán Barú National Park
- Location: Eastern Chiriqui Province, near the Costa Rican border
- How to get there: Fly to David, then take a taxi or shuttle to Boquete (approx. $60-$100)
- Cost of getting there: $60-$100

- Activities/Features: Hiking, camping, birdwatching, and scenic views of the Pacific Ocean and Caribbean Sea
- How to participate: Take a guided hike to the summit, go birdwatching, or camp near the summit
- Cost of participating: $20-$50 for guided hikes, free admission for camping
- Significance: Home to Panama's highest point, with stunning views of both oceans [2]

Coiba Island National Marine Park
- Location: Off the coast of Veraguas Province
- How to get there: Take a domestic flight to Bahia Piña, then a boat to Coiba Island (approx. $200-$300)
- Cost of getting there: $200-$300
- Activities/Features: Snorkeling, scuba diving, whale watching, and dolphin spotting
- How to participate: Take a guided tour or rent equipment for snorkeling or scuba diving
- Cost of participating: $50-$100 for guided tours, $20-$50 for equipment rental
- Significance: A UNESCO World Heritage Site, with an incredible array of marine life [2]

Other National Parks
- Chagres National Park: East of Soberanía National Park, with hiking trails, waterfalls, and wildlife spotting opportunities
- Metropolitan National Park: A urban park in Panama City, with hiking trails, birdwatching, and scenic views of the city
- Isla Bastimentos National Marine Park: A marine park in Bocas del Toro Province, with snorkeling, scuba diving, and whale watching opportunities [3,4]

Hiking and Trekking in Panama: Trails, Guides, and Safety Tips

Here are the details for hiking and trekking in Panama:

Pipeline Road Trail

- _Location_: Soberanía National Park, Panama
- _How to navigate_: The trailhead is located near the Soberanía National Park entrance. Take a taxi or ride-hailing service from Panama City (approx. $10-$20).
- _Cost_: Free admission, but a $5-$10 fee may be charged for parking.
- _Guided tours_: Panama Trails offers guided hikes on the Pipeline Road Trail for $60-$80 per person.
- _Difficulty_: Easy to moderate
- _Duration_: 5-7 hours
- _Features_: Birdwatching, wildlife spotting, and scenic views of the surrounding rainforest.

Volcán Barú Summit Trail

- _Location_: Volcán Barú National Park, Chiriqui Province, Panama
- _How to navigate_: Take a domestic flight from Panama City to David (approx. $100-$200), then a taxi or shuttle to the trailhead (approx. $20-$30).
- _Cost_: $10-$20 admission fee, plus $10-$20 for parking.
- _Guided tours_: Ecocircuitos Panama offers guided hikes to the summit of Volcán Barú for $120-$180 per person.
- _Difficulty_: Challenging
- _Duration_: 8-10 hours
- _Features_: Scenic views of the Pacific Ocean and Caribbean Sea, wildlife spotting, and summiting the highest point in Panama.

Camino de Cruces Trail

- _Location_: Soberanía National Park, Panama
- _How to navigate_: The trailhead is located near the Soberanía National Park entrance. Take a taxi or ride-hailing service from Panama City (approx. $10-$20).
- _Cost_: Free admission, but a $5-$10 fee may be charged for parking.
- _Guided tours_: Panama City Hikers offers guided hikes on the Camino de Cruces Trail for $40-$60 per person.
- _Difficulty_: Moderate
- _Duration_: 4-6 hours
- _Features_: Scenic views of the surrounding rainforest, wildlife spotting, and historic significance as an ancient Spanish colonial road.

El Valle de Antón Trail

- _Location_: El Valle de Antón, Coclé Province, Panama
- _How to navigate_: Take a bus from Panama City to El Valle de Antón (approx. $5-$10), then a taxi or shuttle to the trailhead (approx. $10-$20).
- _Cost_: Free admission, but a $5-$10 fee may be charged for parking.
- _Guided tours_: Ecocircuitos Panama offers guided hikes in El Valle de Antón for $80-$120 per person.
- _Difficulty_: Moderate
- _Duration_: 4-6 hours
- _Features_: Scenic views of the surrounding mountains, wildlife spotting, and exploring the charming town of El Valle de Antón.

Boquete Trails

- _Location_: Boquete, Chiriqui Province, Panama
- _How to navigate_: Take a domestic flight from Panama City to David (approx. $100-$200), then a taxi or shuttle to Boquete (approx. $20-$30).
- _Cost_: Free admission, but a $5-$10 fee may be charged for parking.
- _Guided tours_: Panama Trails offers guided hikes in Boquete for $60-$80 per person.
- _Difficulty_: Easy to challenging
- _Duration_: 2-6 hours
- _Features_: Scenic views of the surrounding mountains, wildlife spotting, and exploring the charming town of Boquete.

Safety Tips

1. _Plan ahead_: Research the trail, check the weather, and bring necessary gear and supplies.
2. _Bring a guide_: Consider hiring a guide or joining a guided tour, especially for more challenging trails.
3. _Stay hydrated_: Bring plenty of water and electrolyte-rich snacks to stay hydrated and energized.
4. _Respect the environment_: Follow park rules, stay on designated trails, and avoid littering or damaging the environment.
5. _Be prepared for emergencies_: Bring a first aid kit, know basic first aid techniques, and have a plan for emergency situations.

Panama's Beaches: A Guide to the Best Beaches on the Pacific and Caribbean Coasts

Here's a comprehensive guide to Panama's best beaches:

Pacific Coast Beaches

1. Playa Coronado

- _Location_: Coronado, Panama
- _How to get there_: Take a taxi or ride-hailing service from Panama City (approx. $40-$60)
- _Navigation route_: From Panama City, take the Pan-American Highway westbound towards Coronado
- _Cost of getting there_: $40-$60
- _Features/activities_: Swimming, sunbathing, surfing, and water sports
- _How to participate_: Rent surfboards or paddleboards, take a surf lesson, or simply relax on the beach
- _Requirements/cost_: No requirements, free admission

2. Playa Farallón

- _Location_: Farallón, Panama
- _How to get there_: Take a taxi or ride-hailing service from Panama City (approx. $60-$80)
- _Navigation route_: From Panama City, take the Pan-American Highway westbound towards Farallón
- _Cost of getting there_: $60-$80
- _Features/activities_: Swimming, sunbathing, snorkeling, and scuba diving

- _How to participate_: Rent snorkeling or scuba diving gear, take a guided tour, or simply relax on the beach
- _Requirements/cost_: No requirements, free admission

3. Playa Santa Clara

- _Location_: Santa Clara, Panama
- _How to get there_: Take a taxi or ride-hailing service from Panama City (approx. $30-$50)
- _Navigation route_: From Panama City, take the Pan-American Highway westbound towards Santa Clara
- _Cost of getting there_: $30-$50
- _Features/activities_: Swimming, sunbathing, kayaking, and paddleboarding
- _How to participate_: Rent kayaks or paddleboards, take a guided tour, or simply relax on the beach
- _Requirements/cost_: No requirements, free admission

Caribbean Coast Beaches

1. Playa Bocas del Toro

- _Location_: Bocas del Toro, Panama
- _How to get there_: Take a domestic flight from Panama City to Bocas del Toro (approx. $100-$200)
- _Navigation route_: From Bocas del Toro Airport, take a taxi or shuttle to the beach (approx. $10-$20)
- _Cost of getting there_: $100-$200
- _Features/activities_: Swimming, sunbathing, snorkeling, scuba diving, and surfing
- _How to participate_: Rent snorkeling or scuba diving gear, take a guided tour, or simply relax on the beach
- _Requirements/cost_: No requirements, free admission

2. Playa Colon
- _Location_: Colón, Panama
- _How to get there_: Take a taxi or ride-hailing service from Panama City (approx. $40-$60)
- _Navigation route_: From Panama City, take the Transisthmian Highway northbound towards Colón
- _Cost of getting there_: $40-$60
- _Features/activities_: Swimming, sunbathing, and water sports
- _How to participate_: Rent water sports equipment, take a guided tour, or simply relax on the beach
- _Requirements/cost_: No requirements, free admission

3. Playa Portobelo
- _Location_: Portobelo, Panama
- _How to get there_: Take a taxi or ride-hailing service from Panama City (approx. $60-$80)
- _Navigation route_: From Panama City, take the Transisthmian Highway northbound towards Portobelo
- _Cost of getting there_: $60-$80
- _Features/activities_: Swimming, sunbathing, snorkeling, and scuba diving

- _How to participate_: Rent snorkeling or scuba diving gear, take a guided tour, or simply relax on the beach
- _Requirements/cost_: No requirements, free admission

Surfing, Snorkeling, and Diving in Panama: Best Spots and Operators

Panama offers a diverse range of surfing, snorkeling, and diving opportunities, from beginner-friendly breaks to challenging reef dives. Here are some of the best spots and operators:

Surfing

1. Playa Venao: A laid-back beach town on the Pacific coast, known for its consistent waves and lively surf scene.
    - Location: Playa Venao, Panama
    - Best for: Beginners and intermediate surfers
    - Operators: Venao Surf School, Playa Venao Surf Camp
    - Cost: Lessons from $30-$50, board rentals from $10-$20
2. Playa Santa Catalina: A world-renowned surf spot on the Pacific coast, known for its powerful waves and stunning scenery.
    - Location: Playa Santa Catalina, Panama
    - Best for: Experienced surfers
    - Operators: Santa Catalina Surf School, Playa Santa Catalina Surf Camp
    - Cost: Lessons from $40-$60, board rentals from $15-$30

Snorkeling

1. Bocas del Toro: An archipelago in the Caribbean Sea, known for its vibrant coral reefs and diverse marine life.
    - Location: Bocas del Toro, Panama

- Best for: Beginners and experienced snorkelers
   - Operators: Bocas del Toro Snorkeling Tours, Red Frog Bungalows
   - Cost: Tours from $50-$80, equipment rentals from $10-$20
2. Portobelo National Park: A protected area on the Caribbean coast, known for its coral reefs and historic shipwrecks.
   - Location: Portobelo National Park, Panama
   - Best for: Beginners and experienced snorkelers
   - Operators: Portobelo Snorkeling Tours, Panama Divers
   - Cost: Tours from $40-$60, equipment rentals from $10-$20

Diving

1. Coiba National Park: A UNESCO World Heritage Site and one of the best diving destinations in the world.
   - Location: Coiba National Park, Panama
   - Best for: Experienced divers
   - Operators: Coiba Dive Center, Panama Divers
   - Cost: Tours from $100-$150, equipment rentals from $20-$30
2. Bocas del Toro: An archipelago in the Caribbean Sea, known for its vibrant coral reefs and diverse marine life.
   - Location: Bocas del Toro, Panama
   - Best for: Beginners and experienced divers
   - Operators: Bocas del Toro Dive Center, Red Frog Bungalows
   - Cost: Tours from $80-$120, equipment rentals from $15-$25

Remember to always dive and snorkel with a certified operator and follow safe diving practices.

Wildlife and Birdwatching in Panama: National Parks, Reserves, and Tours

Panama is a paradise for wildlife and birdwatching enthusiasts, with its unique geography and tropical climate supporting an incredible array of biodiversity. Here are some of the top national parks, reserves, and tours for wildlife and birdwatching in Panama:

National Parks

1. _Soberanía National Park_: A 22,000-hectare park just north of Panama City, home to over 1,000 species of birds, monkeys, sloths, and jaguars.
    - Location: Soberanía, Panama
    - How to get there: Take a taxi or ride-hailing service from Panama City (approx. $10-$20)
    - Cost: $5-$10 admission fee
    - Features: Hiking trails, birdwatching, wildlife spotting

2. _Volcán Barú National Park_: A 14,000-hectare park in western Panama, home to quetzals, toucans, and howler monkeys.
   - Location: Volcán Barú, Panama
   - How to get there: Take a domestic flight from Panama City to David (approx. $100-$200), then a taxi or shuttle to the park (approx. $20-$30)
   - Cost: $10-$20 admission fee
   - Features: Hiking trails, birdwatching, wildlife spotting
3. _Darién National Park_: A 579,000-hectare park in eastern Panama, home to jaguars, pumas, and over 400 species of birds.
   - Location: Darién, Panama
   - How to get there: Take a domestic flight from Panama City to Puerto Obaldia (approx. $150-$300), then a boat to the park (approx. $20-$50)
   - Cost: $20-$30 admission fee
   - Features: Hiking trails, birdwatching, wildlife spotting

Wildlife Reserves

1. _Gamböa Rainforest Reserve_: A 1,000-hectare reserve in central Panama, home to monkeys, sloths, and over 200 species of birds.
   - Location: Gamböa, Panama
   - How to get there: Take a taxi or ride-hailing service from Panama City (approx. $20-$30)
   - Cost: $10-$20 admission fee
   - Features: Hiking trails, birdwatching, wildlife spotting
2. _Punta Patiño Nature Reserve_: A 26,000-hectare reserve in eastern Panama, home to jaguars, pumas, and over 300 species of birds.
   - Location: Punta Patiño, Panama

- How to get there: Take a domestic flight from Panama City to Puerto Obaldia (approx. $150-$300), then a boat to the reserve (approx. $20-$50)
  - Cost: $20-$30 admission fee
  - Features: Hiking trails, birdwatching, wildlife spotting

Birdwatching Tours

1. _Panama Birding Tours_: Offers guided birdwatching tours in Soberanía National Park and other locations.
   - Cost: $80-$120 per person
   - Features: Guided tours, transportation, and equipment
2. _Birds Panama_: Offers guided birdwatching tours in Volcán Barú National Park and other locations.
   - Cost: $100-$150 per person
   - Features: Guided tours, transportation, and equipment

Wildlife Tours

1. _Panama Wildlife Tours_: Offers guided wildlife tours in Soberanía National Park and other locations.
   - Cost: $80-$120 per person
   - Features: Guided tours, transportation, and equipment
2. _Wildlife Panama_: Offers guided wildlife tours in Volcán Barú National Park and other locations.
   - Cost: $100-$150 per person
   - Features: Guided tours, transportation, and equipment

CHAPTER 4: Exploring Panama's Culture and History

Panama's Indigenous Cultures: History, Traditions, and Encounters

Panama is home to seven indigenous groups, each with their own distinct culture, language, and traditions. Here's a comprehensive overview of Panama's indigenous cultures:

History
Panama's indigenous groups have a rich and diverse history that spans over 10,000 years. Here's a brief overview:

1. Pre-Columbian Era: The first indigenous groups arrived in Panama around 10,000 years ago. These groups developed complex societies, with their own systems of government, agriculture, and trade.
2. Spanish Colonization: The arrival of the Spanish in the 16th century had a devastating impact on Panama's indigenous population. Many indigenous people died from diseases brought over by the Spanish, while others were forced to work in mines and on plantations.
3. Independence and Modern Era: After Panama gained independence from Spain in 1821, the government began to recognize the rights of indigenous groups. Today, Panama's indigenous groups continue to fight for their rights and to preserve their cultures.

Traditions
Panama's indigenous groups have a rich cultural heritage, with many traditions and customs that are still practiced today. Here are a few examples:

1. Kuna Textiles: The Kuna people are known for their vibrant textiles, which are woven on looms using traditional techniques. These textiles are highly prized for their beauty and cultural significance.
2. Ngäbe-Buglé Ceramics: The Ngäbe-Buglé people are skilled ceramicists, creating beautiful pots, bowls, and other vessels using traditional techniques.
3. Wounaan Basketry: The Wounaan people are expert basket-makers, creating intricate and beautiful baskets using traditional techniques.
4. Guna Yala Music and Dance: The Guna Yala people have a rich tradition of music and dance, with many different styles and genres. Their music and dance are highly prized for their beauty and cultural significance.

Encounters

Visitors to Panama can experience the country's indigenous cultures firsthand through various encounters. Here are a few examples:

1. Guna Yala Islands: Visitors can stay in traditional Guna Yala villages and experience the local culture. Activities include snorkeling, fishing, and learning about traditional Guna Yala customs.
2. Ngäbe-Buglé Community Tours: Visitors can take guided tours of Ngäbe-Buglé communities, learning about traditional customs and ways of life. Activities include hiking, birdwatching, and traditional crafts.
3. Kuna Textile Workshops: Visitors can take workshops to learn about traditional Kuna textile-making techniques. These workshops provide a unique opportunity to learn about Kuna culture and to create your own traditional textile.
4. Wounaan Basket-Making Workshops: Visitors can take workshops to learn about traditional Wounaan basket-making

techniques. These workshops provide a unique opportunity to learn about Wounaan culture and to create your own traditional basket.

Indigenous Communities to Visit

1. Guna Yala Islands: A archipelago of islands in the Caribbean Sea, home to the Guna Yala people.
2. Ngäbe-Buglé Communities: Communities located in the provinces of Chiriqui and Veraguas, home to the Ngäbe-Buglé people.
3. Kuna Communities: Communities located in the provinces of Panama and Colon, home to the Kuna people.
4. Wounaan Communities: Communities located in the provinces of Chiriqui and Veraguas, home to the Wounaan people.

Responsible Tourism

1. Respect Local Customs: Visitors should respect local customs and traditions, and avoid taking photos or disrupting community activities.
2. Support Local Economies: Visitors should support local economies by purchasing traditional crafts and products, and eating at local restaurants.
3. Protect the Environment: Visitors should protect the environment by avoiding littering, and respecting protected areas and wildlife.

By visiting Panama's indigenous communities and experiencing their cultures firsthand, visitors can gain a deeper understanding and appreciation of the country's rich cultural heritage.

Spanish Colonial History in Panama: Forts, Churches, and Architecture

Panama's Spanish colonial history is a rich and fascinating topic, with many historical sites and landmarks that showcase the country's architectural and cultural heritage. Here are some of the top Spanish colonial historical sites to visit in Panama:

Forts

1. _Fort San Lorenzo_: A 16th-century fort located at the mouth of the Chagres River, which played a crucial role in the defense of the Spanish Main.
    - History: Built in 1597 by the Spanish to protect their treasure fleets from pirate attacks.
    - Structure: A well-preserved fort with thick stone walls, bastions, and a museum.
    - Significance: A UNESCO World Heritage Site and a testament to Panama's rich colonial history.
    - Location: Colon Province, Panama.
    - Navigation: Take a taxi or ride-hailing service from Colon City (approx. $10-$20).
    - Cost implication: $10-$20 admission fee.
    - How to explore: Guided tours available, self-guided exploration also possible.

2. _Fort San Felipe_: A 16th-century fort located in Portobelo, which played a significant role in the Spanish colonization of Panama.
    - History: Built in 1597 by the Spanish to protect their treasure fleets from pirate attacks.
    - Structure: A well-preserved fort with thick stone walls, bastions, and a museum.

- Significance: A UNESCO World Heritage Site and a testament to Panama's rich colonial history.
   - Location: Colon Province, Panama.
   - Navigation: Take a taxi or ride-hailing service from Colon City (approx. $20-$30).
   - Cost implication: $10-$20 admission fee.
   - How to explore: Guided tours available, self-guided exploration also possible.

Churches

1. _San Felipe Church_: A 16th-century church located in Portobelo, which is one of the oldest churches in Panama.
   - History: Built in 1580 by the Spanish.
   - Structure: A well-preserved church with a mix of Spanish colonial and indigenous architectural styles.
   - Significance: A testament to Panama's rich colonial history and cultural heritage.
   - Location: Colon Province, Panama.
   - Navigation: Take a taxi or ride-hailing service from Colon City (approx. $20-$30).
   - Cost implication: Free admission.
   - How to explore: Self-guided exploration possible.

2. _San Jose Church_: A 17th-century church located in Panama City, which is one of the oldest churches in Panama.
   - History: Built in 1671 by the Spanish.
   - Structure: A well-preserved church with a mix of Spanish colonial and indigenous architectural styles.
   - Significance: A testament to Panama's rich colonial history and cultural heritage.
   - Location: Panama City, Panama.
   - Navigation: Take a taxi or ride-hailing service from downtown Panama City (approx. $5-$10).

- Cost implication: Free admission.
   - How to explore: Self-guided exploration possible.

Architecture

1. _Casco Viejo_: A historic neighborhood in Panama City, which features a mix of Spanish colonial, French, and Italian architectural styles.
   - History: Founded in 1671 by the Spanish.
   - Structure: A well-preserved neighborhood with cobblestone streets, historic buildings, and a mix of architectural styles.
   - Significance: A UNESCO World Heritage Site and a testament to Panama's rich colonial history and cultural heritage.
   - Location: Panama City, Panama.
   - Navigation: Take a taxi or ride-hailing service from downtown Panama City (approx. $5-$10).
   - Cost implication: Free admission.
   - How to explore: Self-guided exploration possible, guided tours also available.

2. _Panama Viejo_: A historic site in Panama City, which features the ruins of the original Panama City, founded in 1519 by the Spanish.
   - History: Founded in 1519 by the Spanish.
   - Structure: A well-preserved historic site with ruins of buildings, streets, and a museum.
   - Significance: A UNESCO World Heritage Site and a testament to Panama's rich colonial history and cultural heritage.
   - Location: Panama City, Panama.
   - Navigation: Take a taxi or ride-hailing service from downtown Panama City (approx. $5-$10).

- Cost implication: $10-$20 admission fee.
- How to explore: Guided tours available, self-guided exploration also possible.

The Panama Canal: History, Engineering, and Tourism

History

1. _Early Attempts_: The first attempt to build a canal across the Isthmus of Panama was made by the Spanish in the 16th century. However, the project was abandoned due to engineering challenges and tropical diseases.

2. _French Attempt_: In the late 19th century, the French attempted to build a canal, but they abandoned the project in 1889 due to engineering challenges and financial difficulties.

3. _US Construction_: The United States took over the project in 1904 and completed the canal in 1914. The canal was officially opened on August 15, 1914.

4. _Panamanian Ownership_: The Panama Canal was transferred to Panamanian ownership on December 31, 1999.

Engineering

1. _Locks_: The Panama Canal has three sets of locks: Miraflores, Pedro Miguel, and Gatun. The locks raise and lower ships a total of 85 feet between the two oceans.

2. _Canal_: The canal is approximately 50 miles long and has a minimum depth of 40 feet.

3. _Dams_: The Panama Canal has several dams, including the Gatun Dam, which creates Gatun Lake, the largest artificial lake in the world.

4. _Navigation_: The canal has a complex navigation system, including tugboats, pilots, and a system of buoys and beacons.

Tourism
1. _Panama Canal Tours_: There are several tour operators that offer guided tours of the Panama Canal, including boat tours and visits to the Miraflores Locks Visitor Center.
2. _Miraflores Locks Visitor Center_: The visitor center offers stunning views of the locks and a museum that tells the history of the canal.
3. _Gatun Locks_: Visitors can watch ships pass through the locks and visit the Gatun Locks Visitor Center.
4. _Panama Canal Museum_: The museum is located in the city of Colon and tells the history of the canal from its construction to the present day.

Location
The Panama Canal is located in Panama, Central America, connecting the Atlantic Ocean to the Pacific Ocean.

How to Get There
1. _By Air_: Visitors can fly into Panama City's Tocumen International Airport (PTY) or Colon's Enrique Adolfo Jimenez Airport (ONX).
2. _By Car_: Visitors can drive to the Panama Canal from Panama City or Colon.
3. _By Bus_: Visitors can take a bus from Panama City or Colon to the Panama Canal.

Cost Implications
1. _Panama Canal Tours_: The cost of guided tours of the Panama Canal varies depending on the tour operator and the type of tour. Expect to pay around $50-$100 per person.
2. _Miraflores Locks Visitor Center_: The admission fee to the Miraflores Locks Visitor Center is around $15-$20 per person.
3. _Gatun Locks_: The admission fee to the Gatun Locks is around $10-$15 per person.

Activities
1. _Panama Canal Boat Tours_: Take a guided boat tour of the Panama Canal and see the locks in operation.
2. _Miraflores Locks Visitor Center_: Visit the Miraflores Locks Visitor Center and learn about the history of the Panama Canal.
3. _Gatun Locks_: Watch ships pass through the Gatun Locks and visit the Gatun Locks Visitor Center.
4. _Panama Canal Museum_: Visit the Panama Canal Museum in Colon and learn about the history of the canal.

How to Participate
1. _Book a Tour_: Book a guided tour of the Panama Canal with a reputable tour operator.
2. _Visit the Miraflores Locks Visitor Center_: Visit the Miraflores Locks Visitor Center and learn about the history of the Panama Canal.
3. _Watch Ships Pass Through the Locks_: Watch ships pass through the Gatun Locks or Miraflores Locks.
4. _Take a Boat Tour_: Take a guided boat tour of the Panama Canal and see the locks in operation.

Panama's Vibrant Arts Scene: Museums, Galleries, and Street Art

Panama's vibrant arts scene is a reflection of the country's rich cultural heritage and its position as a hub of creativity and innovation in Central America. Here are some of the top museums, galleries, and street art destinations to explore in Panama:

Museums

1. _Museo de Arte Contemporaneo_: Located in Panama City, this museum features a diverse collection of contemporary art from Panama and around the world.
   - Location: Panama City, Panama
   - Hours: Tuesday - Sunday, 10am - 5pm
   - Admission: $5-$10
2. _Museo Nacional de Panama_: This museum in Panama City showcases the country's history, culture, and natural environment.
   - Location: Panama City, Panama
   - Hours: Tuesday - Sunday, 9am - 4pm
   - Admission: $5-$10
3. _Museo de la Biodiversidad_: Located in Panama City, this museum features interactive exhibits on Panama's natural environment and biodiversity.
   - Location: Panama City, Panama
   - Hours: Tuesday - Sunday, 10am - 5pm
   - Admission: $10-$20

Galleries

1. _Galeria Artefacto_: Located in Panama City, this gallery features contemporary art from Panama and around the world.
   - Location: Panama City, Panama
   - Hours: Monday - Friday, 10am - 6pm
   - Admission: Free
2. _Galeria Tumbaga_: Located in Casco Viejo, Panama City, this gallery features contemporary art from Panama and around the world.
   - Location: Casco Viejo, Panama City, Panama
   - Hours: Tuesday - Sunday, 10am - 6pm

- Admission: Free

3. _Galeria Habana_: Located in Panama City, this gallery features contemporary art from Cuba and around the world.
   - Location: Panama City, Panama
   - Hours: Monday - Friday, 10am - 6pm
   - Admission: Free

Street Art

1. _Casco Viejo_: This historic neighborhood in Panama City is known for its vibrant street art scene, with many colorful murals and graffiti adorning the buildings.
   - Location: Casco Viejo, Panama City, Panama
   - Hours: Always open
   - Admission: Free

2. _El Chorrillo_: This neighborhood in Panama City is known for its vibrant street art scene, with many colorful murals and graffiti adorning the buildings.
   - Location: El Chorrillo, Panama City, Panama
   - Hours: Always open
   - Admission: Free

3. _Calzada de Amador_: This scenic road in Panama City is known for its vibrant street art scene, with many colorful murals and graffiti adorning the buildings.
   - Location: Calzada de Amador, Panama City, Panama
   - Hours: Always open
   - Admission: Free

Festivals and Events

1. _Festival de las Artes_: This annual festival in Panama City celebrates the country's vibrant arts scene, with music, dance, theater, and visual arts performances.
   - Location: Panama City, Panama

- Dates: March - April
   - Admission: Free - $20
2. _Bienal de Panama_: This biennial art festival in Panama City showcases the work of local and international artists, with exhibitions, performances, and workshops.
   - Location: Panama City, Panama
   - Dates: October - November
   - Admission: Free - $20
3. _Feria de las Flores y del Café_: This annual festival in Boquete celebrates the country's coffee and flower industries, with music, dance, and food.
   - Location: Boquete, Panama
   - Dates: January
   - Admission: Free - $10

Festivals and Celebrations in Panama: Calendar, Traditions, and Tips

Panama's festivals and celebrations are a vibrant reflection of its rich cultural heritage. Here are some of the top festivals and celebrations to experience in Panama:

Carnaval de Las Tablas
This four-day celebration, held before Ash Wednesday, is Panama's most massive Carnaval celebration. It features parades, floats, music, dancing, and serious partying in the small town of Las Tablas on the Azuero Peninsula [1] [2].

Fiestas Patrias
Celebrated in November, Fiestas Patrias commemorates Panama's separation from Colombia in 1903. It's a patriotic event featuring parades, music, and traditional dances [1] [2].

Corpus Christi
This Catholic holiday, celebrated in May or June, commemorates the Eucharist. The biggest celebration takes place in La Villa de Los Santos on the Azuero Peninsula, featuring elaborate dances and traditional costumes.

Festival de la Mejorana en Guararé
Held in September, this festival celebrates Panama's folkloric heritage with music, dance, and traditional costumes. It's a great opportunity to experience Panama's rich cultural traditions.

Feria de Flores y Café
This festival, held in January, celebrates Panama's coffee and flower industries. It's a great opportunity to experience Panama's natural beauty and rich cultural heritage.

Semana Santa
Celebrated the week before Easter, Semana Santa is a significant religious holiday in Panama. It features processions, traditional food, and family gatherings.

Festival de Cristo Negro de Portobelo
Held on October 21st, this festival celebrates the Black Christ of Portobelo. It features processions, traditional music, and dance.

National Pollera Festival
Celebrated in July, this festival showcases Panama's traditional pollera dress. It features parades, music, and traditional dances [3].

When attending these festivals, be sure to:

- Book accommodations and tours in advance, as prices tend to increase during peak festival seasons.
- Respect local customs and traditions, especially during religious celebrations.
- Try traditional Panamanian cuisine, such as arroz con pollo, sancocho, and empanadas.
- Learn some basic Spanish phrases to interact with locals and enhance your festival experience.

Overall, Panama's festivals and celebrations offer a unique glimpse into the country's rich cultural heritage. With its vibrant music, colorful costumes, and delicious cuisine, Panama is the perfect destination for festival enthusiasts.

CHAPTER 5: Regional Guides

Boquete: A Guide to Panama's Adventure Capital

1. Open your camera app. This is the built-in camera application that comes with your phone.

2. Point your camera at the QR code. Try to hold your phone steady and make sure the QR code is within the frame, especially if you're using a scanner app.

3. Focus on the QR code. Most camera apps will automatically detect the QR code, but sometimes you might need to tap the screen to focus.

4. A notification or link will appear. Once your phone scans the QR code, you'll usually see a notification or link appear on your screen.

5. Tap the notification or link. This will take you to the webpage, app, or information encoded in the QR code.

Boquete is a charming town located in the Chiriqui Highlands of Panama, known for its stunning natural beauty, pleasant climate, and endless opportunities for outdoor adventure. Here's a comprehensive guide to help you plan your trip to Boquete:

Location and Climate
Boquete is situated in the Chiriqui Highlands, about 60 km (37 miles) northwest of David, the capital city of Chiriqui Province. The town has a mild climate, often referred to as the "Eternal Spring" due to its consistent temperatures ranging from 18°C to 25°C (64°F to 77°F) throughout the year.

Getting There
1. By Air: The nearest airport is Enrique Malek International Airport (DAV) in David, which receives flights from Panama City and other major cities in Central America. From David, you can take a taxi or shuttle to Boquete.
2. By Bus: You can take a bus from Panama City or David to Boquete. The journey takes around 4-5 hours from Panama City and 1-2 hours from David.
3. By Car: Boquete is accessible by car from Panama City or David. The journey takes around 4-5 hours from Panama City and 1-2 hours from David.

Activities and Attractions
Boquete is a paradise for outdoor enthusiasts, offering a wide range of activities and attractions, including:

1. Hiking and Trekking:

Boquete is surrounded by beautiful mountains, forests, and valleys, offering numerous hiking and trekking trails for all levels.

2. Coffee Plantations: Boquete is famous for its coffee, and visiting a coffee plantation is a must-do activity. Learn about the coffee-making process, and sample some of the best coffee in the world.

3. Rafting and Kayaking: The Chiriqui River offers exciting rafting and kayaking opportunities, with rapids ranging from gentle to extreme.

4. Zip Lining: Fly through the jungle canopy on one of Boquete's many zip line tours, offering breathtaking views of the surrounding mountains and valleys.

5. Hot Springs: Relax and rejuvenate in one of Boquete's many natural hot springs, perfect for soothing sore muscles after a day of hiking or adventure activities.

6. Wildlife Watching: Boquete is home to a wide range of wildlife, including monkeys, sloths, toucans, and quetzals. Take a guided tour or venture into the jungle on your own to spot these incredible creatures.

Food and Drink
Boquete is renowned for its delicious cuisine, which combines traditional Panamanian dishes with international flavors. Be sure to try some of the local specialties, including:

1. Coffee: Boquete is famous for its coffee, and you can find numerous coffee shops and cafes throughout the town.
2. Seafood: Boquete is close to the Pacific Ocean, and as a result, you can find an abundance of fresh seafood, including fish, shrimp, and lobster.
3. Traditional Panamanian Cuisine: Try some of the local specialties, such as sancocho (a hearty stew), arroz con pollo (chicken and rice), and empanadas (meat or cheese pastries).

Safety and Precautions
Boquete is generally a safe town, but as with any travel destination, it's essential to take some precautions:

1. Be mindful of your belongings: Keep an eye on your luggage and personal belongings, especially in crowded areas or public transportation.
2. Respect the local environment: Boquete is surrounded by beautiful natural scenery, so be sure to respect the local environment and wildlife.
3. Stay hydrated: Boquete's climate can be hot and humid, so be sure to drink plenty of water throughout the day.

Tips and Insights
1. Learn some Spanish: While many locals in Boquete speak English, learning some basic Spanish phrases can go a long way in enhancing your experience.
2. Be prepared for variable weather: Boquete's weather can be unpredictable, so be sure to pack accordingly and be prepared

for sudden rain showers or cooler temperatures in the evenings.
3. Respect local customs and traditions_: Boquete is a small town with a strong sense of community, so be sure to respect local customs and traditions, especially during festivals and celebrations.
4. Try local transportation_: Boquete has a reliable and affordable public transportation system, including buses and taxis. Try using local transportation to get a feel for the local culture and to support the local economy.
5. Be mindful of your impact on the environment_: Boquete is a popular tourist destination, and as a result, it's essential to be mindful of your impact on the environment. Try to reduce your plastic usage, respect protected areas, and support eco-friendly tour operators.

Events and Festivals

Boquete hosts several events and festivals throughout the year, including:

1. _Boquete Jazz and Blues Festival_: Held annually in February, this festival features live music performances by local and international artists.
2. _Boquete Flower and Coffee Festival_: Held annually in January, this festival celebrates Boquete's famous coffee and flowers, with live music, food, and craft stalls.
3. _Semana Santa_: Held annually in March or April, Semana Santa is a significant religious holiday in Panama, with processions, traditional food, and family gatherings.

Day Trips and Excursions

Boquete is an excellent base for exploring the surrounding countryside and nearby attractions, including:

1. _Volcan Baru National Park_: A scenic drive from Boquete, this national park offers stunning views of the surrounding mountains and valleys, as well as hiking trails and opportunities for birdwatching.
2. _Bocas del Toro_: A scenic drive and ferry ride from Boquete, Bocas del Toro is a popular archipelago with stunning beaches, coral reefs, and a vibrant nightlife.
3. _David_: A scenic drive from Boquete, David is the capital city of Chiriqui Province, with a rich history, cultural attractions, and a vibrant market.

Accommodation Options

Boquete offers a wide range of accommodation options, including:

1. _Luxury Hotels_: Boquete has several luxury hotels, including the Hotel Panamonte and The Haven, which offer comfortable rooms, fine dining, and excellent service.
2. _Boutique Hotels_: Boquete has several boutique hotels, including the Hotel Finca Lerida and the Hotel Casa Grande, which offer comfortable rooms, personalized service, and a unique atmosphere.
3. _Hostels and Guesthouses_: Boquete has several hostels and guesthouses, including the Boquete Hostel and the Guesthouse Casa de Montaña, which offer budget-friendly accommodation, communal kitchens, and a social atmosphere.
4. _Vacation Rentals_: Boquete has several vacation rentals, including apartments, houses, and cabins, which offer self-catering accommodation, flexibility, and a home-away-from-home experience.

TIPS AND INSIGHTS
1. _Respect local customs and traditions_: Boquete is a small town with a strong sense of community, so be sure to respect local customs and traditions, especially during festivals and celebrations.
2. _Try local transportation_: Boquete has a reliable and affordable public transportation system, including buses and taxis. Try using local transportation to get around town and experience the local culture.
3. _Be mindful of your physical limitations_: Boquete offers a wide range of outdoor activities, but be sure to be mindful of your physical limitations and take necessary precautions to avoid injury.

Events and Festivals
Boquete hosts several events and festivals throughout the year, including:

1. _Boquete Flower and Coffee Festival_: Held in January, this festival celebrates Boquete's famous coffee and flowers.
2. _Boquete Jazz and Blues Festival_: Held in February, this festival features live music performances by local and international jazz and blues musicians.
3. _Semana Santa_: Held in March or April, this festival celebrates Holy Week with processions, music, and traditional food.
4. _Feria de Boquete_: Held in June, this festival celebrates Boquete's founding with music, dance, and traditional food.

Day Trips and Excursions
Boquete is a great base for exploring the surrounding countryside and nearby attractions. Some popular day trips and excursions include:

1. _Volcan Baru National Park_: Take a guided hike to the summit of Volcan Baru, Panama's highest peak.
2. _Boquete Canyon_: Explore the scenic Boquete Canyon, which offers stunning views of the surrounding mountains and valleys.
3. _Los Cangilones_: Visit the scenic Los Cangilones, a series of waterfalls and swimming holes.
4. _David_: Take a day trip to David, the capital city of Chiriqui Province, which offers a range of cultural attractions and activities.

By following this guide, you'll be well on your way to experiencing the best of Boquete and its surrounding countryside.

Bocas del Toro: A Guide to Panama's Caribbean Archipelago

Bocas del Toro is a stunning Caribbean archipelago located in the northwest of Panama. The archipelago consists of six main islands, including Isla Colón, Isla Carenero, Isla Bastimentos, Isla Solarte, Isla San Cristóbal, and Isla Popa. Here's a comprehensive guide to help you plan your trip to Bocas del Toro:

Getting There
1. _By Air_: You can fly to Bocas del Toro International Airport (BOC) from Panama City's Tocumen International Airport (PTY) or other major airports in Central America.
2. _By Bus and Boat_: You can take a bus from Panama City to Almirante, and then a boat to Bocas del Toro.
3. _By Private Boat or Yacht_: You can also reach Bocas del Toro by private boat or yacht.

Accommodation
1. _Luxury Resorts_: Bocas del Toro has several luxury resorts, including the Punta Caracol Acqua-Lodge and the Red Frog Beach Island Resort.
2. _Boutique Hotels_: The archipelago also has several boutique hotels, including the Hotel Palma Royale and the Hotel Bocas del Toro.
3. _Hostels and Guesthouses_: For budget-friendly options, consider staying at a hostel or guesthouse, such as the Bocas del Toro Hostel or the Guesthouse Casa de los Abuelos.
4. _Vacation Rentals_: You can also rent apartments, houses, or villas through services like Airbnb or VRBO.

Activities and Attractions
1. _Snorkeling and Scuba Diving_: Explore the stunning coral reefs and marine life of Bocas del Toro.
2. _Surfing and Paddleboarding_: Take advantage of the archipelago's world-class surf breaks and calm waters for paddleboarding.
3. _Fishing_: Go on a fishing tour or try your luck from the shore.
4. _Hiking and Birdwatching_: Explore the islands' lush forests and spot exotic birds.
5. _Visiting Indigenous Communities_: Learn about the culture and traditions of the Ngäbe-Buglé indigenous community.

Food and Drink
1. _Seafood_: Enjoy fresh seafood at one of the many local restaurants.
2. _Traditional Panamanian Cuisine_: Try traditional dishes like sancocho, arroz con pollo, and empanadas.
3. _International Cuisine_: Bocas del Toro also has a range of international restaurants serving everything from Italian to Mexican cuisine.
4. _Fresh Fruits and Vegetables_: Take advantage of the archipelago's fresh produce, including coconuts, mangoes, and pineapples.

Safety and Precautions
1. _Be mindful of your belongings_: Keep an eye on your luggage and personal belongings, especially in crowded areas or public transportation.
2. _Respect the local environment_: Bocas del Toro is a fragile ecosystem, so be sure to respect the local environment and wildlife.

3. _Take necessary precautions for water activities_: Always wear a life jacket and follow safety instructions when engaging in water activities like snorkeling, scuba diving, or surfing.

Tips and Insights
1. _Learn some Spanish_: While many locals in Bocas del Toro speak English, learning some basic Spanish phrases can go a long way in enhancing your experience.
2. _Be prepared for variable weather_: Bocas del Toro has a tropical climate, with sudden rain showers and changes in temperature. Be sure to pack accordingly and stay hydrated.
3. _Respect local customs and traditions_: Bocas del Toro has a rich cultural heritage, with a mix of indigenous, African, and Spanish influences. Be sure to respect local customs and traditions, especially during festivals and celebrations.

Events and Festivals
Bocas del Toro hosts several events and festivals throughout the year, including:

1. _Bocas del Toro Festival_: Held annually in September, this festival celebrates the archipelago's culture, music, and cuisine.
2. _Sea Turtle Festival_: Held annually in October, this festival raises awareness about sea turtle conservation and features live music, food, and activities.
3. _Bocas Jazz Festival_: Held annually in May, this festival features live jazz music performances by local and international artists.
4. _Feria de Bocas del Toro_: Held annually in June, this fair celebrates the archipelago's culture, music, and cuisine, with live performances, food stalls, and craft exhibitions.

Day Trips and Excursions

Bocas del Toro is an excellent base for exploring the surrounding islands and nearby attractions, including:

1. _Island-Hopping Tour_: Take a guided tour to explore the surrounding islands, including Isla Carenero, Isla Bastimentos, and Isla Solarte.
2. _Dolphin Bay_: Visit Dolphin Bay, a secluded beach with crystal-clear waters and a chance to spot dolphins.
3. _Red Frog Beach_: Explore Red Frog Beach, a stunning beach with powdery sand and crystal-clear waters.
4. _Bastimentos National Marine Park_: Visit Bastimentos National Marine Park, a protected area with stunning coral reefs, marine life, and scenic hiking trails.

Practical Information

1. _Currency_: The Panamanian balboa is the local currency, but US dollars are widely accepted.
2. _Language_: Spanish is the official language, but English is widely spoken.
3. _Weather_: Bocas del Toro has a tropical climate, with temperatures ranging from 70°F to 90°F (21°C to 32°C) throughout the year.
4. _Safety_: Bocas del Toro is generally a safe destination, but take normal precautions to protect yourself and your belongings.

By following this guide, you'll be well on your way to experiencing the best of Bocas del Toro and its stunning Caribbean archipelago.

Colón: A Guide to Panama's Northern Province

Colón is a province located in the northern part of Panama, bordering the Caribbean Sea. The province is home to the city of Colón, which is a major commercial center and a popular tourist destination. Here's a guide to help you explore Colón:

History and Culture
Colón has a rich history dating back to the 16th century when it was a major port for the Spanish Empire. The city was also an important center for the construction of the Panama Canal. Today, Colón is a vibrant city with a mix of colonial and modern architecture, and a rich cultural heritage.

Places to Visit
1. _Colón Free Zone_: A major commercial center and one of the largest free zones in the world.
2. _Gatun Locks_: A set of locks that are part of the Panama Canal and offer stunning views of the canal.

3. _Fort San Lorenzo_: A historic fort that was built by the Spanish in the 16th century.
4. _Colón Cathedral_: A beautiful cathedral that was built in the 19th century.
5. _Museum of Bocas del Toro_: A museum that showcases the history and culture of the Bocas del Toro archipelago.

Activities and Excursions
1. _Panama Canal Tour_: Take a guided tour of the Panama Canal and learn about its history and operation.
2. _Gatun Lake Tour_: Take a boat tour of Gatun Lake and enjoy stunning views of the surrounding landscape.
3. _Colón City Tour_: Take a guided tour of Colón city and explore its historic landmarks and cultural attractions.
4. _Beach Day_: Spend a day relaxing on one of Colón's beautiful beaches, such as Playa La Angosta or Playa La Ensenada.
5. _Shopping_: Visit the Colón Free Zone and shop for duty-free goods, including electronics, jewelry, and clothing.

Accommodation
Colón has a range of accommodation options, including:

1. _Luxury Hotels_: The Radisson Colón 2,000 Hotel and Casino and the Hotel Meliá Colón are two of the top luxury hotels in Colón.
2. _Budget-Friendly Hotels_: The Hotel Centroamericano and the Hotel Colón are two budget-friendly options in the city center.
3. _Hostels and Guesthouses_: Colón has several hostels and guesthouses, including the Hostal Casa Grande and the Guesthouse La Estación.

Dining
Colón has a range of dining options, including:

1. _Seafood Restaurants_: Try some of the fresh seafood at one of Colón's many seafood restaurants, such as El Puerto or La Estación.
2. _Traditional Panamanian Cuisine_: Try some traditional Panamanian dishes, such as sancocho or arroz con pollo, at a local restaurant like El Fogoncito or La Casa de la Abuela.
3. _International Cuisine_: Colón also has several international restaurants, including Italian, Chinese, and Indian options.

Safety and Precautions
Colón is generally a safe city, but take normal precautions to protect yourself and your belongings. Be aware of your surroundings, especially in crowded areas or at night. Avoid carrying large amounts of cash and use reputable taxi services.

Getting Around
Colón has a range of transportation options, including:

1. _Taxis_: Taxis are widely available in Colón and can be hailed on the street or booked in advance.
2. _Public Transportation_: Colón has a public transportation system, including buses and minivans, that connect the city center with outlying neighborhoods and nearby towns.
3. _Rental Cars_: Rental cars are available at the Colón airport or in the city center.

By following this guide, you'll be well on your way to exploring the best of Colón and its surroundings.

Chiriquí: A Guide to Panama's Western Highlands

Chiriquí is a province located in the western highlands of Panama, bordering Costa Rica to the west. The province is known for its stunning natural beauty, rich cultural heritage, and outdoor adventure opportunities. Here's a guide to help you explore Chiriquí:

Places to Visit
1. Boquete: A charming town located in the Chiriquí Highlands, known for its natural beauty, outdoor adventure opportunities, and coffee plantations.
2. Volcán Barú National Park: A national park located near Boquete, featuring stunning hiking trails, scenic views, and opportunities to spot wildlife.
3. David: The capital city of Chiriquí Province, known for its rich cultural heritage, historic landmarks, and vibrant nightlife.

4. Gualaca: A charming town located in the Chiriquí Highlands, known for its natural beauty, outdoor adventure opportunities, and traditional crafts.

Activities and Excursions
1. Hiking and Trekking: Explore the stunning hiking trails of Volcán Barú National Park and the Chiriquí Highlands.
2. Coffee Tours: Visit coffee plantations in Boquete and learn about the coffee-making process.
3. Rafting and Kayaking: Enjoy whitewater rafting and kayaking in the Chiriquí River and surrounding streams.
4. Birdwatching: Spot exotic bird species in the Chiriquí Highlands and Volcán Barú National Park.

Accommodation
1. Luxury Hotels: The Hotel Panamonte and The Haven are two luxury hotels located in Boquete, offering comfortable rooms, fine dining, and excellent service.
2. Boutique Hotels: The Hotel Finca Lerida and the Hotel Casa Grande are two boutique hotels located in Boquete, offering comfortable rooms, personalized service, and a unique atmosphere.
3. Hostels and Guesthouses: Boquete and David have several hostels and guesthouses, offering budget-friendly accommodation, communal kitchens, and a social atmosphere.

Dining
1. Traditional Panamanian Cuisine: Try traditional Panamanian dishes, such as sancocho, arroz con pollo, and empanadas, at local restaurants in Boquete and David.
2. International Cuisine: Boquete and David have several international restaurants, offering everything from Italian to Mexican cuisine.

3. Fresh Produce: Take advantage of the fresh produce available in the Chiriquí Highlands, including fruits, vegetables, and dairy products.

Safety and Precautions
1. Be mindful of your belongings: Keep an eye on your luggage and personal belongings, especially in crowded areas or public transportation.
2. Respect the local environment: The Chiriquí Highlands are a fragile ecosystem, so be sure to respect the local environment and wildlife.
3. Take necessary precautions for outdoor activities: Always wear protective gear and follow safety instructions when engaging in outdoor activities like hiking, rafting, or kayaking.

Getting Around
1. Rent a Car: Rent a car in David or Boquete to explore the Chiriquí Highlands and surrounding areas.
2. Public Transportation: Use public transportation, including buses and minivans, to get around the Chiriquí Highlands and surrounding areas.
3. Taxis: Use taxis to get around David and Boquete, or to travel to nearby towns and attractions.

Darién: A Guide to Panama's Eastern Wilderness

Darién is a province located in the eastern part of Panama, bordering Colombia to the east. The province is known for its vast wilderness, diverse wildlife, and rich cultural heritage. Here's a guide to help you explore Darién:

Places to Visit

1. _Darién National Park_: A UNESCO World Heritage Site and one of the most biodiverse places on the planet, featuring stunning hiking trails, scenic views, and opportunities to spot wildlife.
2. _Guna Yala_: An indigenous reserve located along the Caribbean coast, known for its stunning beaches, crystal-clear waters, and vibrant cultural heritage.
3. _Puerto Obaldia_: A small town located on the Caribbean coast, known for its stunning beaches, scenic views, and opportunities to spot wildlife.
4. _Metetí_: A small town located in the heart of Darién, known for its rich cultural heritage, traditional cuisine, and opportunities to explore the surrounding wilderness.

Activities and Excursions

1. _Hiking and Trekking_: Explore the stunning hiking trails of Darién National Park and the surrounding wilderness.
2. _Wildlife Spotting_: Spot exotic wildlife, including monkeys, sloths, toucans, and quetzals, in Darién National Park and the surrounding wilderness.
3. _Indigenous Community Visits_: Visit indigenous communities, such as the Guna and Wintu, and learn about their traditional way of life, culture, and customs.
4. _Fishing and Boating_: Enjoy fishing and boating in the Caribbean Sea and the surrounding rivers and streams.

Accommodation

1. _Eco-Lodges_: Stay in eco-lodges, such as the Darién Eco-Lodge or the Punta Patiño Lodge, which offer comfortable

accommodation, stunning views, and opportunities to explore the surrounding wilderness.

2. _Indigenous Community Lodges_: Stay in indigenous community lodges, such as the Guna Yala Lodge or the Wintu Lodge, which offer traditional accommodation, cultural experiences, and opportunities to learn about indigenous customs and traditions.

3. _Camping_: Camp in the wilderness of Darién National Park or the surrounding areas, which offer stunning views, opportunities to spot wildlife, and a chance to disconnect from the modern world.

Safety and Precautions

1. _Be mindful of your belongings_: Keep an eye on your luggage and personal belongings, especially in crowded areas or public transportation.

2. _Respect the local environment_: Darién is a fragile ecosystem, so be sure to respect the local environment and wildlife.

3. _Take necessary precautions for outdoor activities_: Always wear protective gear and follow safety instructions when engaging in outdoor activities like hiking, fishing, or boating.

Getting Around

1. _Rent a 4x4 Vehicle_: Rent a 4x4 vehicle to explore the rugged terrain of Darién and the surrounding areas.

2. _Public Transportation_: Use public transportation, including buses and minivans, to get around Darién and the surrounding areas.

3. _Boats and Ferries_: Use boats and ferries to travel along the Caribbean coast and explore the surrounding islands and communities.

CHAPTER 6: Practical Information and Safety Tips

Safety and Security in Panama: Tips, Precautions, and Emergency Contacts

Panama is generally a safe country to visit, with low crime rates compared to other Central American countries. However, as with any travel destination, it's essential to take necessary precautions to ensure your safety and security. Here are some tips, precautions, and emergency contacts to help you stay safe in Panama:

General Safety Tips

1. Be aware of your surroundings: Pay attention to your environment, especially in crowded areas or tourist hotspots.
2. Keep valuables secure: Keep your valuables, such as your passport, cash, and credit cards, secure and out of sight.
3. Use reputable transportation: Use licensed taxis or ride-sharing services, and always check the driver's ID before getting in.
4. Avoid traveling alone at night: Try to avoid traveling alone at night, especially in rural areas or unfamiliar neighborhoods.
5. Stay informed: Stay up-to-date with local news and events that may affect your safety.

Specific Safety Concerns

1. Petty theft: Petty theft, such as pickpocketing or bag snatching, is a common crime in tourist areas. Be mindful of your belongings, especially in crowded areas.

2. Scams: Scams, such as credit card scams or fake tours, are common in tourist areas. Be cautious when using ATMs or credit cards, and research tour operators before booking.
3. Traffic accidents: Traffic accidents are a common cause of injury and death in Panama. Be careful when crossing streets, and always wear a seatbelt when driving or riding in a vehicle.
4. Natural disasters: Panama is prone to natural disasters, such as hurricanes, floods, and earthquakes. Stay informed about weather conditions and follow local instructions in case of an emergency.

Emergency Contacts
1. Panama National Police: 104 (emergency number)
2. Tourist Police: 511-9266 (phone number)
3. Panama Red Cross: 507-315-1818 (phone number)
4. US Embassy in Panama: 507-317-5000 (phone number)
5. Canadian Embassy in Panama: 507-294-2500 (phone number)

Staying Safe in Specific Areas
1. Panama City: Be cautious in crowded areas, such as the Casco Viejo neighborhood, and avoid walking alone at night.
2. Colón: Be mindful of your belongings, especially in crowded areas, and avoid walking alone at night.
3. Boquete: Be cautious when hiking or trekking, and always follow local instructions and guidelines.
4. Bocas del Toro: Be mindful of your belongings, especially in crowded areas, and avoid swimming alone in remote areas.

By following these safety tips, being aware of specific safety concerns, and knowing who to contact in case of an emergency, you can have a safe and enjoyable trip to Panama.

Health and Medical Care in Panama: Vaccinations, Hospitals, and Insurance

Panama offers a high standard of medical care, with modern hospitals and medical facilities, especially in Panama City and other major urban areas. Here's a guide to help you navigate health and medical care in Panama:

Vaccinations
1. Routine Vaccinations: Make sure you're up-to-date on all routine vaccinations, including MMR, DTaP, polio, and influenza.
2. Recommended Vaccinations: The Centers for Disease Control and Prevention (CDC) recommend the following vaccinations for travel to Panama:
   - Hepatitis A
   - Hepatitis B
   - Typhoid
3. Other Vaccinations: Depending on your specific travel plans and activities, you may also want to consider vaccinations for:
   - Rabies (if you plan to spend time around animals)
   - Yellow fever (if you plan to visit areas with a high risk of yellow fever transmission)

Hospitals and Medical Facilities
1. Panama City: Panama City has several high-quality hospitals, including:
   - Hospital Punta Pacífica
   - Hospital Nacional
   - Clínica Paitilla
2. Other Cities: Other major cities in Panama, such as David and Colón, also have modern hospitals and medical facilities.

3. Rural Areas: Medical facilities in rural areas may be more limited, so it's essential to plan ahead and research medical options before traveling to these areas.

Medical Insurance
1. Travel Insurance: Consider purchasing travel insurance that covers medical expenses, including evacuation and repatriation.
2. Health Insurance: If you're a resident in Panama, you may want to consider purchasing health insurance that covers medical expenses in Panama and abroad.
3. Reciprocal Health Agreements: Panama has reciprocal health agreements with some countries, including the United States, Canada, and several European countries. These agreements may provide access to medical care at reduced costs or with reduced paperwork.

Health Concerns
1. Zika and Dengue Fever: Panama has reported cases of Zika and dengue fever, so take necessary precautions to prevent mosquito bites.
2. Chikungunya: Panama has also reported cases of chikungunya, a viral disease transmitted by mosquitoes.
3. Water and Food Safety: Take necessary precautions to ensure safe drinking water and food, especially when eating at street vendors or in rural areas.

Additional Tips
1. Research Medical Facilities: Research medical facilities and hospitals in your destination and make a list of emergency contact numbers.
2. Pack a First-Aid Kit: Pack a first-aid kit with essentials, such as pain relievers, antacids, and bandages.

3. Stay Informed: Stay informed about local health concerns and outbreaks, and take necessary precautions to stay safe.

Transportation in Panama: Buses, Taxis, and Rental Cars

Panama has a well-developed transportation system, with various options available for getting around, including buses, taxis, and rental cars. Here's a guide to help you navigate transportation in Panama:

Buses
1. Public Buses: Public buses are an affordable and efficient way to get around Panama. They operate on a network of routes, including urban and intercity routes.
2. Express Buses: Express buses are a faster option for intercity travel, with fewer stops and more comfortable seating.
3. Tourist Buses: Tourist buses are designed for tourists, offering a more comfortable and secure way to travel. They often operate on popular routes, such as Panama City to Boquete.

Taxis
1. Yellow Taxis: Yellow taxis are the most common type of taxi in Panama. They are metered, but it's always a good idea to agree on the fare before you start your journey.
2. Radio Taxis: Radio taxis are a safer and more reliable option, as they are dispatched through a central system and have GPS tracking.
3. Uber and Ride-Hailing Apps: Uber and other ride-hailing apps operate in Panama, offering a convenient and affordable way to get around.

Rental Cars
1. Car Rental Companies: Several car rental companies operate in Panama, including international brands like Hertz and Avis.
2. Driving Requirements: To rent a car in Panama, you'll need a valid driver's license from your home country and a credit card.
3. Road Conditions: Panama's roads are generally in good condition, but you may encounter some rough roads or construction delays, especially in rural areas.

Other Transportation Options
1. Domestic Flights: Domestic flights operate between major cities in Panama, including Panama City, David, and Bocas del Toro.
2. Ferries: Ferries operate between Panama City and nearby islands, as well as between other coastal towns.
3. Bicycles and Scooters: Bicycles and scooters are a great way to get around Panama City and other urban areas.

Safety Tips
1. Be Aware of Your Surroundings: Always be aware of your surroundings, especially in crowded areas or at night.
2. Use Reputable Transportation Services: Use reputable transportation services, such as licensed taxis or ride-hailing apps.
3. Wear a Seatbelt: Always wear a seatbelt when traveling by car or bus.

Transportation Costs
1. _Bus Fares_: Bus fares in Panama are relatively affordable, with prices starting from around $1-$2 for a local bus ride.

2. _Taxi Fares_: Taxi fares in Panama are also relatively affordable, with prices starting from around $5-$10 for a short ride.

3. _Rental Car Costs_: Rental car costs in Panama vary depending on the type of vehicle and rental duration, but expect to pay around $40-$100 per day.

4. _Domestic Flight Costs_: Domestic flight costs in Panama vary depending on the route and airline, but expect to pay around $100-$300 for a one-way ticket.

Transportation Tips for Tourists

1. _Learn Some Spanish_: While many Panamanians speak some English, learning some basic Spanish phrases can go a long way in helping you navigate the transportation system.

2. _Use Reputable Transportation Services_: Use reputable transportation services, such as licensed taxis or ride-hailing apps, to ensure your safety.

3. _Be Prepared for Delays_: Be prepared for delays, especially during rush hour or in areas with heavy construction.

4. _Respect Local Customs_: Respect local customs and traditions, especially when traveling to rural areas or interacting with indigenous communities.

Transportation Infrastructure

1. _Highways_: Panama has a well-developed highway system, with several major highways connecting the country's main cities.

2. _Public Transportation_: Panama has a comprehensive public transportation system, including buses and taxis, which cover most areas of the country.

3. _Airports_: Panama has several international airports, including Tocumen International Airport in Panama City, which offer connections to major cities around the world.

4. _Ports_: Panama has several major ports, including the Port of Panama City and the Port of Colón, which handle a significant portion of the country's trade.

Future Transportation Projects
1. _Panama Metro_: The Panama Metro is a rapid transit system currently under construction in Panama City, which will provide a convenient and efficient way to travel around the city.
2. _High-Speed Rail_: There are plans to build a high-speed rail line connecting Panama City to other major cities in the country, which will reduce travel times and improve connectivity.
3. _Airport Expansions_: Several airports in Panama are undergoing expansions, including Tocumen International Airport, which will increase capacity and improve facilities for passengers.

By understanding the transportation options and infrastructure in Panama, you can plan your trip more effectively and make the most of your time in this beautiful country.

Communication in Panama: Language, Phone, and Internet

Communication is a vital aspect of any trip, and Panama offers a range of options for staying connected. Here's a guide to help you navigate communication in Panama:

Language
1. _Official Language_: Spanish is the official language of Panama.

2. _English_: English is widely spoken, especially in tourist areas, major cities, and among businesspeople.

3. _Indigenous Languages_: Several indigenous languages are also spoken in Panama, including Ngäbere, Buglé, and Kuna.

Phone

1. _Mobile Network Operators_: Panama has several mobile network operators, including Claro, Digicel, and Movistar.

2. _SIM Cards_: You can purchase SIM cards from mobile network operators or convenience stores.

3. _International Calls_: International calls can be made from public phones or mobile phones.

4. _Phone Codes_: The country code for Panama is +507, and the area code for Panama City is 2.

Internet

1. _Internet Cafes_: Internet cafes are widely available in tourist areas and major cities.

2. _Wi-Fi_: Many hotels, restaurants, and cafes offer free Wi-Fi.

3. _Mobile Data_: Mobile data plans are available from mobile network operators.

4. _Internet Speed_: Internet speeds in Panama are generally fast, with average speeds ranging from 10-50 Mbps.

Postal Services

1. _Correos y Telégrafos Nacionales_: Correos y Telégrafos Nacionales is the national postal service of Panama.

2. _Post Offices_: Post offices are located throughout the country, including in major cities and tourist areas.

3. _Mail Delivery_: Mail delivery times vary depending on the destination, but generally take 3-7 days within Panama and 7-14 days internationally.

Other Communication Options
1. _Radio_: Radio is a popular form of communication in Panama, with several stations broadcasting in Spanish and English.
2. _Television_: Television is also widely available in Panama, with several channels broadcasting in Spanish and English.
3. _Newspapers_: Several newspapers are published in Panama, including La Prensa, El Panama América, and The Panama News.

By understanding the communication options available in Panama, you can stay connected with family and friends back home, navigate the country with ease, and make the most of your trip.

Responsible Travel in Panama: Environmental Impact, Cultural Sensitivity, and Community Support

Panama is a country with a rich cultural heritage and a diverse natural environment. As a responsible traveler, you can play a significant role in preserving the country's natural beauty and cultural traditions. Here are some tips on how to travel responsibly in Panama:

Environmental Impact
1. _Reduce Plastic Use_: Refuse single-use plastics, such as straws, bags, and water bottles. Instead, opt for reusable alternatives.
2. **_Conserve Water_**: Take shorter showers and turn off the tap while brushing your teeth to conserve water.
3. _Respect Wildlife_: Keep a safe distance from wildlife, and never touch or feed them.

4. _Support Eco-Tourism_: Choose tour operators that follow sustainable tourism practices and support conservation efforts.

Cultural Sensitivity
1. _Learn About Local Customs_: Research local customs and traditions to avoid unintentionally offending locals.
2. _Respect Indigenous Communities_: Be respectful of indigenous communities and their traditions. Ask permission before taking photos or visiting sacred sites.
3. _Support Local Artisans_: Purchase local handicrafts and support artisans to promote cultural preservation.
4. _Learn Some Spanish_: Make an effort to learn some basic Spanish phrases to show respect for the local culture.

Community Support
1. _Support Local Businesses_: Choose local businesses, such as family-run restaurants and small shops, to support the local economy.
2. _Volunteer_: Consider volunteering with local organizations or conservation projects to give back to the community.
3. _Respect Local Ways of Life_: Be respectful of local ways of life and traditions. Avoid disrupting local activities or events.
4. _Support Sustainable Tourism Initiatives_: Look for tourism initiatives that support sustainable tourism practices and community development.

By following these tips, you can help preserve Panama's natural beauty and cultural heritage, while also supporting local communities and promoting sustainable tourism practices.

Appendix

Panama's Map

Geography
Panama is a country located in Central America, bordering Costa Rica to the west and Colombia to the east. It has a total area of approximately 75,417 square kilometers (29,119 square miles).

Regions
Panama can be divided into several regions, including:

1. Panama City:

PANAMA CITY

SCAN THE QR CODE

1. Open yo l'veur camera app. This is the built-in camera application that comes with your phone.

2. Point your camera at the QR code. Try to hold your phone steady and make sure the QR code is within the frame, especially if you're using a scanner app.

3. Focus on the QR code. Most camera apps will automatically detect the QR code, but sometimes you might need to tap the screen to focus.

4. A notification or link will appear. Once your phone scans the QR code, you'll usually see a notification or link appear on your screen.

5. Tap the notification or link. This will take you to the webpage, app, or information encoded in the QR code.

The capital city, located on the Pacific coast.

2. Colón:

COLON

SCAN THE QR CODE

1. Open your camera app. This is the built-in camera application that comes with your phone.

2. Point your camera at the QR code. Try to hold your phone steady and make sure the QR code is within the frame, especially if you're using a scanner app.

3. Focus on the QR code. Most camera apps will automatically detect the QR code, but sometimes you might need to tap the screen to focus.

4. A notification or link will appear. Once your phone scans the QR code, you'll usually see a notification or link appear on your screen.

5. Tap the notification or link. This will take you to the webpage, app, or information encoded in the QR code.

A city located on the Caribbean coast, near the Panama Canal.

3. Chiriquí:

Chiriquí

SCAN THE QR CODE

1. Open your camera app. This is the built-in camera application that comes with your phone.

2. Point your camera at the QR code. Try to hold your phone steady and make sure the QR code is within the frame, especially if you're using a scanner app.

3. Focus on the QR code. Most camera apps will automatically detect the QR code, but sometimes you might need to tap the screen to focus.

4. A notification or link will appear. Once your phone scans the QR code, you'll usually see a notification or link appear on your screen.

5. Tap the notification or link. This will take you to the webpage, app, or information encoded in the QR code.

A province located in the western highlands, known for its coffee plantations and volcanic landscapes.

4. Bocas del Toro:

Bocas del Toro

SCAN THE QR CODE

1. Open your camera app. This is the built-in camera application that comes with your phone.

2. Point your camera at the QR code. Try to hold your phone steady and make sure the QR code is within the frame, especially if you're using a scanner app.

3. Focus on the QR code. Most camera apps will automatically detect the QR code, but sometimes you might need to tap the screen to focus.

4. A notification or link will appear. Once your phone scans the QR code, you'll usually see a notification or link appear on your screen.

5. Tap the notification or link. This will take you to the webpage, app, or information encoded in the QR code.

An archipelago located in the Caribbean Sea, known for its beautiful beaches and coral reefs.

5. Darién:

SCAN THE QR CODE

1. Open your camera app. This is the built-in camera application that comes with your phone.

2. Point your camera at the QR code. Try to hold your phone steady and make sure the QR code is within the frame, especially if you're using a scanner app.

3. Focus on the QR code. Most camera apps will automatically detect the QR code, but sometimes you might need to tap the screen to focus.

4. A notification or link will appear. Once your phone scans the QR code, you'll usually see a notification or link appear on your screen.

5. Tap the notification or link. This will take you to the webpage, app, or information encoded in the QR code.

A province located in the eastern part of the country, known for its dense rainforests and indigenous communities.

Borders
Panama shares borders with:

1. Costa Rica: To the west.
2. Colombia: To the east.

Coastlines
Panama has coastlines on:

1. Pacific Ocean: To the south.
2. Caribbean Sea: To the north.

This is a brief overview of Panama's map.

Spanish Phrases for Travelers

Here are some essential Spanish phrases for travelers:

Basic Phrases
1. _Hola_ (OH-lah): Hello
2. _Buenos días_ (BWEH-nohs DEE-ahs): Good morning
3. _Buenas tardes_ (BWEH-nahs TAR-dehs): Good afternoon
4. _Buenas noches_ (BWEH-nahs NOH-chehs): Good evening
5. _Adiós_ (ah-DEE-yos): Goodbye
6. _Gracias_ (GRAH-see-ahs): Thank you
7. _Por favor_ (pohr fah-VOHR): Please
8. _Lo siento_ (LOH see-en-toh): Excuse me / Sorry
9. _¿Cómo estás?_ (KOH-moh eh-STAH): How are you?
10. _Estoy bien_ (eh-STOH bee-EHN): I'm fine

Travel-Related Phrases
1. _¿Dónde está...?_ (DOHN-deh eh-STAH): Where is...?

2. _¿Cuánto cuesta?_ (KWAHN-toh KWEHS-tah): How much does it cost?

3. _Un billete, por favor_ (oon bee-LAY-tay pohr fah-VOHR): A ticket, please

4. _¿Dónde puedo encontrar...?_ (DOHN-deh pweh-DAH ehn-tehn-ah-RAH): Where can I find...?

5. _Un taxi, por favor_ (oon TAHK-see pohr fah-VOHR): A taxi, please

6. _¿Cuál es el mejor camino?_ (KWAH-al ehs el meh-YOHR kah-MEE-noh): Which is the best way?

7. _Un mapa, por favor_ (oon MAH-pah pohr fah-VOHR): A map, please

8. _¿Dónde está el baño?_ (DOHN-deh eh-STAH el BAH-nyoh): Where is the restroom?

Food and Drink

1. _Un café, por favor_ (oon kah-FAY pohr fah-VOHR): A coffee, please

2. _Un vaso de agua, por favor_ (oon vah-zoh deh AH-gwah pohr fah-VOHR): A glass of water, please

3. _La carta, por favor_ (lah KAHR-tah pohr fah-VOHR): The menu, please

4. _Un plato de..._ (oon PLAH-toh deh): A plate of...

5. _La cuenta, por favor_ (lah KWEHN-tah pohr fah-VOHR): The bill, please

Emergency Phrases

1. _Ayuda_ (ah-YOO-dah): Help

2. _Emergencia_ (eh-mehr-HEHN-see-ah): Emergency

3. _Policía_ (poh-LEE-see-ah): Police

4. _Hospital_ (oh-spi-TAH-lee): Hospital

5. _¿Dónde está el hospital más cercano?_ (DOHN-deh eh-STAH el oh-spi-TAH-lee MAH-say SEHR-kah-noh): Where is the nearest hospital?

Panama's Currency and Exchange Rates

Panama's official currency is the Panamanian balboa (PAB), but interestingly, the US dollar is also widely accepted and used in the country. In fact, the Panamanian balboa is pegged to the US dollar on a one-to-one basis, meaning that one balboa is equivalent to one US dollar [1].

As for exchange rates, since the Panamanian balboa is pegged to the US dollar, the exchange rate remains constant at 1:1. However, if you're looking to exchange your money to or from other currencies, such as the Nigerian naira (NGN), the exchange rates can fluctuate. For example, as of the current exchange rate, 1 PAB is equivalent to approximately 1,630.87 NGN [2].

Here are some current exchange rates for the Panamanian balboa:

- 1 PAB = 1 USD (constant rate due to pegging)
- 1 PAB = 0.000651924 EUR (as of the current exchange rate)

Keep in mind that exchange rates can fluctuate frequently, so it's always a good idea to check the current rates before making any transactions

Emergency Contacts and Important Phone Numbers

Here are some emergency contacts and important phone numbers to keep handy when traveling to Panama:

Emergency Services

1. _Police_: 104
2. _Fire Department_: 103
3. _Ambulance_: 102
4. _National Emergency Number_: 911

Government Offices

1. _Panama Tourism Authority_: +507 526-7000
2. _Panama Immigration Office_: +507 507-1800
3. _Panama Customs Office_: +507 507-3300

Embassies and Consulates

1. _US Embassy in Panama_: +507 317-5000
2. _Canadian Embassy in Panama_: +507 294-2500
3. _UK Embassy in Panama_: +507 297-6550

Medical Services

1. _Hospital Punta Pacífica_: +507 204-8000
2. _Hospital Nacional_: +507 207-8100
3. _Clínica Paitilla_: +507 265-8800

Other Important Numbers

1. _Directory Assistance_: 113
2. _International Operator_: 106
3. _National Operator_: 105

Remember to keep these numbers handy, especially in case of an emergency. It's also a good idea to make digital copies of these numbers and store them in your phone or cloud storage.

CONCLUSION

Panama, a country of incredible diversity and beauty, offers a unique and unforgettable experience for travelers. From the vibrant streets of Panama City to the tranquil beaches of Bocas del Toro, and from the lush rainforests of Darién to the majestic Panama Canal, there's no shortage of exciting destinations and activities to explore.

Throughout this book, we've provided you with a comprehensive guide to Panama, covering everything from transportation and accommodation to culture and cuisine. We've also shared valuable tips and insights to help you navigate the country like a local.

As you prepare to embark on your Panamanian adventure, remember to be open-minded, curious, and respectful of the local culture and environment. Take time to appreciate the little things, engage with the friendly locals, and soak up the laid-back atmosphere.

Whether you're a seasoned traveler or just starting to explore the world, Panama has something for everyone. So pack your bags, grab your camera, and get ready to experience the adventure of a lifetime in this incredible country.

¡Disfruta tu viaje a Panamá! (Enjoy your trip to Panama!)